What should I feed my baby?

Other cookery titles from Spring Hill, an imprint of How To Books:

THE EVERYDAY FISH COOKBOOK
Simple, delicious recipes for cooking fish
Trish Davies

EVERYDAY THAI COOKING
Easy, authentic recipes from Thailand to cook for friends and family
Siripan Akvanich

THE EVERYDAY HALOGEN FAMILY COOKBOOK
Sarah Flower

MAKE YOUR OWN ORGANIC ICE CREAM
Using home grown and local produce
Ben Vear

THE HEALTHY LIFESTYLE DIET COOKBOOK
Sarah Flower

Write or phone for a catalogue to:

How To Books
Spring Hill House
Spring Hill Road
Begbroke
Oxford
OX5 1RX
Tel. 01865 375794

Or email: info@howtobooks.co.uk

Visit our website www.howtobooks.co.uk to find out more about us and our books.

Like our Facebook pages **How To Books** and **Spring Hill Books**

Follow us on **Twitter @Howtobooksltd**

Read our books online www.howto.co.uk

What should I feed my baby?

Introducing your child and family to life-long healthy eating

PURE EBBA

SPRING HILL

Special thanks to my mentor and my good friend Raw Solla (www.rawsolla.com). With a heart of gold, she makes the best recipes and food ever.

And also to my parents who have always done everything they think can help me and benefit me in any way. To have parents like that is like winning the lottery. I am so grateful.

And to my husband and children who always stand by me and love me just the way I am. They make me want to become a better person.

And to my friends and loved ones ... love you all, thank you for being in my life.

Published by Spring Hill, an imprint of How To Books Ltd
Spring Hill House, Spring Hill Road, Begbroke, Oxford OX5 1RX United Kingdom
Tel: (01865) 375794, Fax: (01865) 379162, info@howtobooks.co.uk www.howtobooks.co.uk

Based on the book: Hva∂ á ég a∂ gefa barninu mínu a∂ bor∂a?
by Ebba Gudny Gudmundsdottir, published in 2007 and 2009

First published 2013

British Library Cataloguing in Publication Data. A catalogue record of this book is available from the British Library.

ISBN: 978 1 908974 06 8

Produced for How To Books by Deer Park Productions, Tavistock, Devon
Designed and typeset by Mousemat Design Ltd
Photographs by Ragna Sif Thorsdottir; Golli; Arni Torfason and Hjordis Vigfusdottir
Edited by Wendy Hobson
Printed and bound by Graficas Cems, Villatuerta (Spain)

Contents

Dear Parents

I truly hope this book will help you feed your precious baby nutritious food, making your child happy and healthy. I also hope it will encourage everybody else in your family to eat a healthier diet, and in doing so experience how good it tastes, how easy it is and how it benefits you in every way. I believe that it improves our quality of life to eat a varied diet of fresh, natural products instead of processed, dead food. How can such food give us life and energy when it is lifeless itself?

Following a healthy diet isn't always easy; nobody eats healthy food all the time (I don't). So be kind to yourself when you are tired, overwhelmed or simply feeling a bit under the weather. Taking good care of your baby is hard work! But what you will discover very quickly is that you have much more energy, physically and mentally, when you eat nutritious food. You will also start looking your best.

All the best to you all and I hope I will see you at www.pureebba.com, on Facebook and Twitter!

Sincerely yours

Ebba

Breastfeeding

It is currently recommended by the World Health Organization that babies drink nothing but breast milk until they have reached a full 6 months of age. This is because breast milk is an extremely concentrated food with exactly the right amount and balance of nourishment (vitamins, minerals, fats, and so on) for babies. It is also very easily digested and utilised by their delicate gastrointestinal tract.

To breastfeed successfully, the mother needs support, plenty of rest and as little stress as possible; it's already stressful trying to get to know a small baby who depends upon you entirely! The mother also has to eat well herself and drink plenty of water. Some foods are particularly good for a lactating mother – as for everybody else, of course – such as dark green and orange vegetables, organic coconut water and herbal teas like fennel and chamomile. It is also especially important for both pregnant women and lactating mothers to get enough of fatty acids like omega-3, from krill oil or purified fish oil, which is an excellent source of EPA and DHA, two essential fatty acids. Plant sources of omega-3 include chia seeds, hemp seeds, flax seeds, walnuts and acai. But essential raw fats in general are very beneficial, so eat avocados, almonds, seeds and nuts, pure almond, hazelnut and macadamia nut butter (which tastes great with apples, for instance) and smoothies made from almonds, tahini, seeds and nuts. (There are recipes in this book and how-to videos on my website www.puréebba.com). Personally, I also sometimes eat organic cream and butter.

I also want to mention the grain quinoa, which is extremely nourishing and has an especially high mineral and protein content (and you'll find recipes in this book). The healthy Spelt Waffles on page 183 served me well when I was breastfeeding my children. I always had waffle dough in my fridge and could bake myself a healthy waffle whenever I felt oh-so-hungry but had little time to prepare anything. Salads are also a great option, dressed with a good salad dressing (and there is one in this book, as you may guess!) and some nuts, seeds, dried fruit, avocado and anything else you like and have in your fridge.

All mothers should make sure they get plenty of vitamin B, especially B12, iron, vitamin D (from sunshine), omega-3 as well as other essential fatty acids, magnesium and zinc, along with other vitamins and minerals. Vegan mothers should be particularly careful to ensure they get sufficient vitamin B12, as this is mainly found in animal products.

Any lactating mother with a sweet tooth should definitely try the Healthy and Delicious Chocolate Mousse on page 182, made from avocado, banana and coconut oil; you won't believe how tasty it is – it takes you to heaven! The shakes on pages 116–125 are also wonderful for virtually all human beings, let alone tired mothers. And remember that vitamin D is also important. We get this from the sun so let the sun shine on your bare skin for about 1–2 hours a week or use supplements when there is little sun where you live.

There are lots of recipes in this book that will benefit nursing mums – all made from whole, living foods. And I promise they will help you to have a better, happier life!

The advantages of breastfeeding

Apart from the obvious advantages outlined above, there are other very positive aspects to breastfeeding that everybody may not be aware of.

For the baby

- Breast milk contains antibodies to illnesses the mother has had, which offer increased protection to her baby against infections and can also reduce the risk of allergies.
- The first substance from the mother's breast, the colostrum, helps the baby pass meconium (a newborn's first stools) and thus reduces the risk of jaundice. It also contains many properties that support the baby's immune system.
- Suckling at the breast enhances good hand-eye co-ordination and also promotes proper jaw and teeth alignment.
- Babies absorb the iron in the breast milk well due to the presence of vitamin C and specialised proteins.
- Breast milk responds to the needs of the baby; it is a living, constantly changing food. For example, the milk produced for a premature baby is very different from the breast milk produced

for a full-term infant. And even the milk that flows at the beginning of a feed is more watery than the milk that comes out towards the end of the feeding, which is much richer in fat. Both are vital for the baby. It's almost like magic!

For the mother

- Breastfeeding immediately after the birth helps to contract the uterus.
- A lactating mother has to consume around an extra 500 kcal per day. In my experience, breastfeeding definitely aids in weight loss – it really shrinks you (yay!) and I loved being able to eat more!
- The hormone prolactin, which is produced in the mother as a result of breastfeeding, is a relaxant. It is said to help promote maternal feelings and therefore help the mother and baby to bond.
- Studies show that breastfeeding reduces the mother's risk of developing breast cancer.
- Breastfeeding saves time and money. Formula feeding is expensive.
- Outings with your baby are much easier when you can feed your baby with naturally hygienic breast milk. You don't have to worry about bottles, heating, sterilising, and so on – very convenient to say the least!
- Mothers have to sit and rest while feeding, which helps them to maintain their strength and avoid becoming over-tired.
- Breastfeeding encourages a feeling of closeness between mother and baby that is amazing.

Other alternatives

Having said that, I know that many women have trouble breastfeeding their children, for many different reasons. And I want to tell all the mothers who cannot breastfeed their baby, despite really wanting to, that I know oh so many truly great people who were never breastfed or breastfed only for a short period of time (myself included!). So don't waste your precious hours on guilt and self-punishment. Some things are just not meant to be and life isn't always straightforward. Hey, it wouldn't be fun if it was and nobody gets it all, so no worries, just smile and enjoy life and your precious little baby ... you'll never get this special time back.

No breast milk?

If a mother cannot breastfeed her child for any reason and needs to feed her baby formula milk, there are organic options available so make the best choice you can, depending on what is available. Please be aware that rice milk, soya milk, oat milk or other similar products cannot be used as a substitute for breast milk or organic baby formulas.

It is important to be extremely accurate when making the formula. Follow the instructions to the letter. If the formula is too concentrated (not enough liquid, too much formula powder), it can put too much strain on the baby's digestive system and kidneys. On the other hand if there is too much water, it might not be nourishing enough for a growing child (so the baby will lack essential vitamins and minerals).

Babies who are breastfed get the healthy bacteria needed for the perfect functioning of their digestive system with their mother's milk. If you are not breastfeeding your child, you can buy infant acidophilus in a powder form in health stores. Keep it in a refrigerator and put 1/2 tsp in the formula 1–3 times a day, depending on the age and weight of the baby and following the instructions on the packet closely. It is very important for all of us to have lots of healthy bacteria in our gut. Our immune system and digestion work better and we are much more able to absorb the vitamins and minerals we are consuming. It also helps with bowel discharge.

It is very easy and very common to completely forget yourself and your relationship with your partner when you have a baby. Having a baby is wonderful and amazing (but, truth be told, it is not always very romantic). It can make the world of difference to a relationship if parents take just a little time here and there to go and see a movie together or go out for dinner, take a walk, have a chat about something other than the baby ... whatever! Even before the baby is born, make a point of finding a babysitter you know well and trust. That way, you will be ready to take opportunities to be a couple as well as a family.

Starting Solids

When the baby is around 6 months of age, it is usually recommended that parents start feeding them solid food, and most will be showing signs that they are ready to move on. All babies are unique, so they will all be ready at slightly different times; and formula-fed babies are more likely to need to start eating solids earlier. Breast milk, or formula, still plays an important role, however, and should be continued until at least the age of one, if possible, most mothers gradually phasing it out as they increase the baby's solid food. Mothers can, of course, breastfeed their children for as long as they are comfortable.

There are a few reasons why it is considered wise to wait until they are 6 months old before starting to give solids to a baby. One is so that the baby can tell you when he or she has had enough by turning their head away from the food. This is an important habit to establish from the start. It is good to stop eating when your stomach tells you it is full, and obviously it is much easier to overfeed a baby who cannot let you know whether or not it is full. Some also argue that it is more likely that babies can become intolerant to certain foods if they are given solids too early. If there is a history of allergies in either of the parents' families, the parents should consult with a doctor or other health care practitioner on what to feed and when, and what to avoid.

Another important reason is that babies are usually born with enough iron in their system to last the first 6 months. Iron is extremely important in the body as it ensures that the immune system can work properly. After 6 months, babies need to obtain iron from their food. Breast milk contains iron in very small quantities and, although it is utilised very efficiently by the body, by the time the baby is 6 months old, assuming it was born on the due date, its iron stores will be depleted. This also means that it is particularly important to monitor the iron stores of babies who were born prematurely, especially when they reach one year of age. Iron deficiency is one of the most common nutritional problems worldwide, although rarely a problem among babies fed a diet of natural foods.

In general, eating solid food is a skill the baby has to master,

when they are ready, and when their digestive system is mature enough to cope with the new foods.

What do you need to make baby food?

Now we'll look at what you need in the kitchen to be able to make baby food and other healthy treats. I like to have a few things in the kitchen ... well, truth be told, I am a complete nut when it comes to kitchen appliances! I trust you can all decide for yourselves how much of this stuff you actually need.

- Small, 500ml Pyrex glass measuring jug, which is perfect for making small quantities of baby food.
- Hand-held blender (this is a must, I tell you!).
- High-speed blender (make sure it is very powerful).
- Food processor (this is not essential as you can use your hand-held blender for most things, and not necessary if you also have a high-speed blender).
- Measuring spoons, a set of scales and a measuring jug.
- A small, sharp knife for peeling an apple, for example.
- A vegetable peeler.
- Two or more cutting boards. You can very well use the same cutting board for raw fruits, vegetables and bread; buy a coloured board if you like. But NEVER cut raw meat on the same board; buy a different colour for raw meat.
- A steamer to steam vegetables, making sure that it fits on your saucepans.
- Spatula.
- One good casserole and one large cooking pot.
- Ice cube trays (free from BPA, etc. – see the note on page 22).
- Freezer bags.
- Sieve.
- Milk nut bag (to sieve almond milk).

And now you are good to go!

I have around four pots in different sizes and one pan in my kitchen. I do not recommend Teflon (I suggest you Google that one to find out more). I love ceramic cookware but I also use stainless steel. Ceramic cookware does not leak anything bad into your food while you are cooking in it.

A note on plastic bottles and microwaves

Take care when buying and using plastic products. Plastic can contain hazardous substances – such as BPA, which mimics oestrogen – which leak into the food it contains. It is even more dangerous when we put hot food into a plastic container, not to mention putting plastic in a microwave.

It is possible to buy plastic bottles, pacifiers and all kinds of plastic containers that do not contain these unwanted substances (such as Bisphenol-A (BPA), phthalates and PVC). You can also use glass containers, which is my preference, wherever possible. So check out products before you buy them.

I also want to warn parents against heating food for their children (or themselves) in a microwave. Many studies have demonstrated that food loses a lot of its nutrients when microwaved, and it even changes its construction (which does not sound good at all!). However, if you are adamant about using a microwave for cooking, I think it would be wise to use glass or ceramic containers. But honestly, when you get used to it, heating food using a stove isn't any more difficult or time consuming. If you want to find out more about plastic and these substances, you can research on the internet but do always go to reputable sources.

There are lots of videos on my website, www.puréebba.com, that show you how to make various dishes and give you lots of hints and tips for healthy eating.

Is your baby ready for solids?

From the age of 6 months to approximately 16 months, babies' taste buds are developing and therefore it is extremely sensible, and beneficial for your baby, if you use that time well and introduce your growing baby to as much healthy, natural food as possible. In that way, you are definitely also limiting the risk of raising a fussy eater (although there are no guarantees!).

You will know when your baby is ready for more than just breast milk, although it may happen at different times for different babies. Here are a few hints as to whether your child is ready to start on solids.

- Your baby is at least 4 months old.
- Your baby has doubled its birth weight.
- Your baby can sit upright and lean forward to reach for things, which in this case would be more food, and back away or turn their head when full.
- Your baby has started wanting more breast milk more frequently.
- The baby shows interest in food other people are eating.
- Your baby starts waking up in the middle of the night and seems to be hungry but has until then slept well through the night.
- In some cultures, it is believed that the appearance of teeth is a sign that the baby is ready for solid foods (although many babies have teeth earlier and some not until they are one).

How to wean your baby

When you start weaning your baby it is good to keep a few things in mind. Most important is to remember that there is no need to hurry because your baby is still getting all the nutrients needed from breast milk or formula. The transition to solid food as the primary source of nutrition should be long and slow. Remember, babies are only used to liquid food, so weaning them is the process of gradually taking them from liquid to solid. At first, most babies only know how to swallow milk, and do not know how to push the food to the back of their mouth and swallow – it's a learning process. So the first foods should be more like thick milk. The closer they are to 6 months, the sooner your baby will learn to swallow.

I advocate introducing your baby to a sustainable organic wholefood diet of living natural foods, and you will see I will talk about different aspects of this throughout the book.

Preparation

- You always start with just one simple whole food; I will explain this in more detail on page 36. Feed the same thing for several days so your baby learns about its taste, then move on to another food.
- The food should be very well puréed and even sieved to make sure it has no chunks in it (not even small ones!) and is very thin to begin with so it is more easily digested and so the baby can easily swallow it.

- Make sure there are NO lumps in the food.
- I always recommend ripe fruits as they are sweeter and easiest to digest.
- Always check the temperature of the food before you feed it to your baby. It is good to put food on the inside of your wrist to check that the food is at body temperature. If it feels warm, it is too hot. It can be colder but not warmer.
- At first you only feed your baby 2–6 tsp of ready-made food once a day. You can dilute the food with breast milk, formula and/or cool boiled water. If you use breast milk or formula, the baby will be tasting something familiar.
- Even though parents might not like some particular food, it doesn't mean their baby won't like it. Our babies are not used to what we are used to. They have their own unspoiled taste buds and I'd like to believe they have a flavour for pure nature. So please do not fall into the trap of not giving your baby something healthy just because you don't like it yourself.

When to feed

- It is sensible to start feeding your baby new types of food at midday rather than late in the day. If your baby's digestive system or body does not tolerate it well, you won't be staying up late with a crying baby.
- Give the first few feeds when your baby is not too hungry. Babies cannot usually swallow everything right away so it can be frustrating if they are too hungry.

Stay relaxed

- The key to success is a relaxed atmosphere and happy approach! Please prepare yourself for disappointment. Perhaps your child does not want to eat or is not quite ready for it. Maybe your baby will take a little time to get used to new flavours. Sometimes it takes a while before they get the hang of pushing the food back and swallowing. Try to judge what the baby is ready for. If the baby is really not interested, wait a few days and try again.
- Children instinctively respond to our behaviour, facial expressions and approach to things. If we are relaxed and smiling, everything will go much more smoothly. This is also a

good approach to follow generally, not just when weaning – when we have to give them medicine or something they might dislike, for example. And a little applause when things go well often does wonders to reinforce good behaviour.

How to start

- It is a good idea at first to start the feed with a little breast milk or formula and then give the solids. You could then end the meal with breast milk or formula.
- Use a soft spoon and begin by putting just a tiny amount on the tip of the spoon. Gently rest the tip of the spoon in their mouth and they will try to suck the food off the spoon. It will take time for them to work out how it's done, but that's all right – just try to use the spoon to scrape the food off the chins, mouth, bib, and so on, then try putting it again into your baby's mouth!
- Make sure you do not overfeed your baby. Ideally, they should be sitting up so they can tell you when they've had enough by turning their head or leaning backwards, which they cannot do when reclining backwards.

Moving on

- After a few weeks (time differs between babies, some sooner, others later) of giving one meal a day, you can increase the feeding of solid foods to two small meals a day.
- However, if your child does not like eating solid foods, don't let feeds become a constant struggle. Simply stop the feeding for a week or so to give both of you a break. Just stick with your usual breast milk or organic formula. Then make a fresh start when you feel you are both ready.
- Some believe that babies should also be allowed to feed themselves as early as possible. It might be quite a messy approach but babies love it; they want to touch as well as taste their food and should definitely be allowed to have a go. The sooner they start to practise, the quicker they will learn so spread a cloth or paper on the floor and let them get messy! It can also keep them a little bit busy during meals, which can be good sometimes!
- As the baby progresses, you can increase the amount you feed, always being careful not to overfeed. Also at around 9 months

(and sooner if your baby likes chewing), it is a good idea to begin to mash the food by hand when possible, instead of puréeing it, to get your baby used to new and coarser food textures.

Initially, babies are only trying to figure out how to place the food at the back of their mouths and swallow it. Also, their digestive system is being trained to digest solid foods rather than just milk. This takes time, practice and patience. Babies usually only eat around 1–2 tbsp food to begin with. The baby should tell you when he or she has had enough by turning their head, leaning back or simply losing all interest. Listen to and observe your child and respond accordingly.

Foods to introduce from 6 months

It is important to introduce new foods to babies only when their digestive systems are able to tolerate them. These lists show you when you could start to introduce particular foods to your growing baby. Bear in mind that health-related research constantly brings new discoveries and test results to light, so I recommend keeping an eye on the latest findings.

If your baby needs to start eating solids earlier than 6 months (like four or five months) you can still use the the following list.

Apple, preferably organic (steamed)
Avocado, ripe
Baby rice cereal made from brown rice or sweet brown rice
Banana, ripe
Buckwheat cereal for babies, which is naturally gluten-free
Butter, organic
Carrots, preferably organic (steamed or juiced)
Cinnamon
Coconut oil, cold-pressed
Coconut water, pure organic
Cream, unsalted organic
Hemp oil, cold-pressed
Linseed oil, cold-pressed
Maize cereal for babies, preferably organic, which is naturally gluten-free

Mango, ripe
Millet cereal for babies
Olive oil, cold-pressed
Papaya
Pears, preferably organic (steamed)
Pineapple
Plums (steamed)
Pumpkin (steamed)
Quinoa cereal for babies, which is naturally gluten-free
Squash, butternut (steamed)
Squash, winter (steamed)
Sunflower oil, cold-pressed
Sweet potato (steamed)
Vanilla, organic powder

Foods to introduce from 7 months

Apple, raw
Apricots, dried
Blueberries, preferably organic
Broccoli (steamed)
Cauliflower (steamed)
Dates
Dried fruits, sulphur free (soaked first for an hour to soften)
Goji berries, sulphur free (soaked first for an hour to soften)
Green beans (boiled)
Oat milk, for the porridge, for example
Parsnip (steamed)
Peach, ripe
Potato (steamed)
Prunes
Pumpkin seed oil, cold-pressed
Rice milk, organic
Tahini, organic white (sesame butter)
Turnip (steamed)

Foods to introduce from 8 months

Apricot

Basil
Bread, yeast-free organic, made from wholegrains, like
spelt/kamut, or from gluten-free grains like buckwheat, millet, rice
or maize
Chia seeds
Coriander (very nourishing)
Cucumber (peeled to begin with – for the first year or so)
Fish (steamed)
Grapes, preferably organic
Ground seeds and sieved seed milk
Melon
Mint
Parsley
Plums

Foods to introduce from 9 months

If there is a peanut allergy in the family you should wait longer than
9 months to give the baby almonds and longer than one year to give
nuts in general. Ask a certified healthcare professional for advice.
Almond butter, pure organic
Almond milk
Almond oil, cold-pressed
Beans of all kinds (well cooked and mashed)
Brussel sprouts (steamed)
Celeriac (steamed)
Celery
Coconut milk, without additives
Courgette (raw or steamed)
Green salad, preferably organic (can be mixed with fruits,
vegetables, beans and so on in purées)
Ground almonds
Kale
Leek
Lentils
Meat, preferably organic, (well cooked, puréed with water and
pushed through a sieve) but I don't recommend pork
Oatmeal cereal for babies
Onion

Pasta, wholegrain organic or gluten-free (soft boiled)
Raspberries
Sesame oil, cold-pressed
Sweet peppers (in stews and soups)

Foods to introduce from 12 months

By the time the baby reaches one year old, they will have a much broader scope of foods and should ideally be moving towards eating a version of the course you have prepared for yourself.

Agave nectar, raw organic, in moderation
Barley cereal for babies
Ginger
Honey, raw organic in moderation

> Uncooked honey sometimes contains botulinum toxins in amounts that are detrimental to infants so do not give honey to a baby who is under a year old.

Kiwi
Lemon
Lime
Maple syrup, organic in moderation
Milk, organic full fat
Nectarine
Nuts and nut milk (ground or blended in smoothies) but I do not recommend peanuts for children
Orange
Pineapple
Pomegranate
Red beetroot (steamed and in moderation as it contains nitrates)
Spinach, preferably organic (steamed and in moderation as it contains nitrates (do not reheat cooked spinach)
Spirulina, organic
Strawberries, organic
Tomatoes
Walnut oil
Yoghurt, organic full fat

Wholegrain and baby porridges

Whole grains (that is, unrefined grains) are highly nutritious. Refined grains, like white wheat which is often bleached, no longer contain all the good nutrients and can therefore not by any means be the base of our daily nourishment. I use organic, whole and unrefined grains. I also think it is great to include a variety of grains in our diet and not to forget the gluten-free ones. I prefer to use gluten-free grains for babies for the first 10–12 months, and quinoa is a favourite. Parents can now buy whole grains of all sorts – quinoa, rice, millet, oats, barley, spelt, buckwheat, amaranth, maize – finely milled and suitable for babies, although do remember to check the list of ingredients on the label to make sure there is nothing else in there.

Most of the time, all you have to do is add hot water or maybe in some cases boil the finely milled grains in water for a couple of minutes – it couldn't be simpler. The ratio is always one part grains to two parts water. You can also soak finely milled grains, like buckwheat and oats, overnight in water or milk (use organic rice milk and later almond milk or organic cow s milk) in a bowl in your fridge and then it is enough just to warm it a little in a small saucepan in the morning.

Whole grains are relatively cheap in comparison to many other types of food (especially unhealthy ones!) and they keep well. They can be taken out and boiled into a nice hot porridge whenever you wish. I therefore want to emphasise how great it is to keep on giving children, as they grow older, porridges made from various grains. And how easy, fulfilling and nourishing they are, too. Often when babies outgrow their baby porridge and want to start chewing, their parents stop giving porridges altogether and just bring on the yoghurt, white bread, white pasta, pastries, milk, and so on, when it is so easy to make such a wonderful porridge. In my home, for example, we like a porridge made with brown rice, dates, organic rice milk or cows' milk, vanilla powder, cinnamon and a little palm sugar. And you won't be surprised that we also love quinoa porridge with lovely lemon-infused olive oil and chunks of apple or mango (page 139), as well as the wonderfully warming oat porridge with organic rice milk or cows' milk, cinnamon, almonds and apples (page 137). The same goes for all the porridge recipes I have given

in this book: nutritious, very easy to make, and delicious for the whole family. It is all about having a clock in your kitchen; the casserole and the stove will do all the work for you!

From my own experience I can safely say that a person eats less when eating whole grains than refined ones. The body feels full much sooner when it is taking in nutritious food with enough protein, good fat, fibre and other essential nutrients. Therefore it is much easier to keep oneself and one's family at a healthy weight when eating whole grains and other whole foods instead of processed grains and other processed foods. Exceptions don't matter – don't worry about them!

As mentioned before many whole grains are naturally gluten-free, including amaranth, buckwheat, maize, millet, quinoa and rice. Gluten is a common allergen that you will not have to worry about if you are feeding your baby these grains.

There are endless possibilities of what to put into baby porridges. Parents can put fruit purées or vegetable purées into them along with some nice organic cold-pressed oil or organic butter or cream (1–2 tsp) so the baby gets enough energy through the meal, which is very important. There is more about healthy fat and its necessities on pages 42–46.

Whole grains versus processed grains

There is no question that there is a huge nutritional difference between whole grains and the processed grains used in many food products. Just look at the labels for the clues. The word 'enriched' means that more than a dozen natural nutrients have been destroyed during processing and a few synthetic ones have been replaced in unnatural proportion. If a food is labelled 'fortified', on the other hand, it indicates that nutrients have been added that were never there in the first place. Sounds fishy to me!

Take wholewheat as an example. Wholewheat kernels look very similar to brown rice before being milled into wholewheat flour.

- The bran (wheat bran) is about 14 per cent of the wheat kernel. It contains almost all of the fibre, some minerals, vitamin B and a little incomplete protein.
- The germ (wheat germ) is less than 3 per cent of the wheat

kernel, but it contains almost all of its nutrients, including protein, iron, vitamin B, zinc, magnesium, vitamin E and unsaturated fatty acids or oils. The germ is the seed of the wheat plant and contains the stuff to grow new life.

- The endosperm is 83 per cent of the wheat kernel. It is almost all starch with very few nutrients. White flour is made from the endosperm.

> When we buy organic and sustainable wholefoods, we are voting for the best for our babies in every respect – from their individual health to the health of our soil, our waters and seas, and our planet.

White flour is the stuff from which most commercial breads, rolls, biscuits, cookies, cakes, muffins and hundreds of other foods are made. So why do manufacturers go to the trouble of removing the germ and the bran? It is simply because white flour has an almost indefinite shelf life since it is lifeless (dead!). The oils in the wheat germ go rancid and get bitter and spoil quickly after the wholewheat kernel has been milled into wholewheat flour. We have a bad habit of demanding a long shelf life for food, which is actually an unfair demand and definitely not a healthy one. Food that is whole and alive spoils (ages!) – it is as simple as that. Some food manufacturers go even further and chemically bleach the wheat to make it even whiter and prettier. So here you have one more good reason to read the list of ingredients and never blindly trust the big letters on the front label.

> Rice can be constipating and so it is good, as your baby starts eating a greater variety of foods, to keep feeding them a variety of grains, and gradually to introduce new whole grains as well as new fruits, new vegetables, cold-pressed oils, almonds, seeds, lentils and beans. Variety is always good in terms of getting all the vitamins and minerals we need since each food is unique. See page 217 if your baby is suffering from constipation.

Aim for variety

As a mother of two, I recommend parents to use the time well from 6 months to 16 months and introduce as many healthy foods as possible in order to try and lay a good foundation in eating habits for the future and also to try to combat fussiness when it comes to eating. It is a good idea to try at least one new food every week because that gradually builds up the variety. Eating as many different foods as possible means nutritional variety since every food is unique.

It is such a wonderful thing to be able to raise your baby on good-quality wholefoods from the start. Everyone recognises the truth of the old saying 'old habits die hard', so you are giving your baby a valuable gift that will last them a lifetime.

About Allergies

Another reason to introduce one new food or flavour at a time is so that you can monitor whether your baby has an allergic reaction to specific types of food. If you are feeding your baby one new type of food every day for four or five days before introducing the next one, you will easily spot any adverse reactions and know the cause. When all goes well – as it will for most babies – then you can introduce the next food. You feed your baby that food (and maybe the food you have already tried) for the next four to five days after that, and on it goes just like that.

If you are concerned that you or your partner suffer from allergies, or an allergy runs in the immediate family (parents and/or siblings), it is a good idea to check with a certified healthcare practitioner before you start weaning your baby. It is also sensible to stick with these whole grains to begin with as they do not contain the potential allergen gluten:

- Quinoa
- Buckwheat
- Rice
- Maize
- Millet
- Amaranth

In such cases, it is also wise to be extra careful when introducing new foods to a baby and especially the common allergens.

Symptoms of food intolerance

No child is the same and certainly no reaction to a food is the same so you need to be observant of anything that is unusual for your child when you introduce a new food. These are common reactions so you may find your child displays one or more of these symptoms, but do be reassured that *most* babies will take to solid food without any such reactions.

- Anxiety
- Blood in stools

- Constipation
- Coughing
- Cramps
- Diarrhoea
- Eczema
- Gas
- Headache
- Hyperactive behaviour
- Itching
- Mouth ulcers
- Nausea
- Rashes
- Runny nose
- Shock
- Swollen eyes
- Swollen lips
- Tiredness
- Vomiting
- Weakness

Some babies need to drink a little when eating. In this case, boiled water cooled to lukewarm is good for them. At first you might just give them a little bit on a soft baby spoon. Water is essential to help with digestion but is actually best drunk between meals instead of with meals so as to not dilute the important digestive fluids. However, a few sips with your meal is just fine. It is also good for the teeth to rinse them by drinking a little water after a meal. Calcium interferes with the body's ability to absorb iron so it is not good to drink calcium-rich drinks (like milk) or fortified calcium drinks with iron-rich food. On the other hand, vitamin C enhances iron absorption. It is my belief that we are doing our children a world of good when we only give them plain water to drink. Organic fruit juices should be given only as a treat and always well diluted.

Common allergens

All these substances are known potential allergens. It is sensible to read the list of ingredients when buying something new so you know exactly what you are about to buy.

- Additives (like aspartame, artificial flavours and colours, MSG, nitrates and preservatives)

- Beans
- Beef
- Citrus fruits
- Eggs
- Fish and shellfish
- Gluten in grains like wheat, barley, oats, spelt and rye
- Kiwi
- Milk products
- Onions
- Peanuts
- Pork
- Strawberries
- Sugar, white
- Tofu
- Tomatoes

It is a very good idea to keep a diary of what you feed your child every day and how your baby behaves in terms of sleep, stools and anything else you notice different (good and bad) and think is important to write down. Then you can very easily notice if some specific food might be causing an allergic reaction in your baby.

Soya products

I have read a lot about soya products, and it is safe to say that references do not all agree, which can be confusing. Firstly, soya products are often highly processed, which is never good. Some people also say that it is not safe to recommend soya products for boys, especially under 2 years of age. This is because soya contains isoflavones, which act in the body like the female hormone oestrogen. If you are concerned, I recommend that you ask your doctor or research this further from reliable sources so that you can make an informed decision.

No matter how healthy food is thought to be, always monitor how your baby reacts to new food. It is a good idea, especially in the beginning, to introduce one new food at a time for a few days and see how the baby reacts to it.

Natural Living Organic Foods

I advocate a diet of natural, organic food – but what do those terms mean in practice?

Organic means that foods are grown according to very strict production guidelines. Organic products and other ingredients are grown without the use of pesticides, synthetic fertilisers, sewage sludge, genetically modified organisms or ionizing radiation. Animals that produce organic meat, poultry, eggs, and dairy products are not given antibiotics or growth hormones. Furthermore, while conventionally produced foods and other items commonly contain artificial colours and ingredients, organic items are not allowed to contain anything artificial. Last but not least, the production of genetically modified crops is not allowed in organic farming.

Different regulations are in force in different regions. In the European Union, regulations 834/2007 and 889/2008 define the specifics of organic food production. The USDA National Organic Program (NOP) definition of organic is a clear and simple outline:

Organic food is produced by farmers who emphasise the use of renewable resources and the conservation of soil and water to enhance environmental quality for future generations. Organic meat, poultry, eggs, and dairy products come from animals that are given no antibiotics or growth hormones. Organic food is produced without using most conventional pesticides; fertilisers made with synthetic ingredients or sewage sludge; bioengineering; or ionizing radiation. Before a product can be labelled 'organic', a government-approved certifier inspects the farm where the food is grown to make sure the farmer is following all the rules necessary to meet USDA organic standards. Companies that handle or process organic food before it gets to your local supermarket or restaurant must be certified too.

In most countries, organic food production is strictly monitored and rigorous certification procedures are in place before a product can be labelled as 'organic'.

Organic farming relies on the action of biological agents like worms, insects and other organisms to maintain soil fertility. Nitrogen is added naturally by growing plants such as clover, and other nutrients come from natural compost and seaweed. This results in healthy soil which, in turn, results in healthy plants. Crops are also rotated to maintain soil fertility and to prevent the build up of insects, diseases and weeds.

- When livestock is organically farmed, the highest possible care is taken to preserve the natural behaviour of the animals. Cows and chickens are allowed to move freely outdoors in the fresh air where they are fed a natural diet and are well cared for. The manure of these healthy animals is used on plants. No artificial fertilisers, pesticides or other are used, resulting in pure water and an unpolluted ecosystem.

Many organic farms have been smaller and family-run in the past, which means that organic food used to be available only at farmer's markets or co-ops. To me, organic is the future, or there will be no future for us and our children on this earth.

What are natural living foods?

Natural living foods are grown without chemical fertilisers and pesticides. This applies to organic foods, of course, but many non-organic foods are also grown in this way.

- They are not genetically modified.
- Animals are not given any added growth hormones, antibiotics or other drugs.
- They do not contain anything artificial or any preservatives.
- They are whole foods, meaning they do not have a long list of ingredients (for example, a high-quality organic pure almond butter should only contain almonds, preferably raw with perhaps some sea salt but no added sugars, oils or other ingredients). When you are buying new products, it is best to read the list of ingredients first.
- They are fresh. This means that if you have the choice between an imported organic product and a fresh local product, the latter is the better option. You can always ask your local farmer how he grows his products.
- They are grown in accordance with the laws of nature. This

means that animals are fed their native, natural diets, rather than a mix of grains or animal by-products, and have free-range access to the outdoors.

- They are grown in a sustainable way. Sustainability rests on the principle that we must meet the needs of the present without compromising the ability of future generations to meet their own needs. This means using minimal amounts of water, protecting the soil from depletion of nutrients, and turning animal waste into natural fertilisers rather than environmental pollutants. Furthermore, it takes into account of social responsibilities such as the working and living conditions of the workers, the needs of rural communities, and consumer health and safety both in the present and the future.
- They do not come from a factory farm.

> What helps keep our immune system healthy:
> The sun and vitamin D
> Omega-3s
> Iron
> Acidophilus (healthy intestinal flora)
> Gratefulness, forgiveness, love, laughter and happy, positive thoughts

Fats

Partly because of the problem of obesity, fats get a bad press, and certainly a healthy balanced diet is low in processed fats! However, we do need fat in our diet, and it is important to understand what kind of fats are bad and what kind are actually very good and essential for us.

Essential fatty acids

We need to consume the essential fatty acids, or EFAs, omega-3s and omega-6s because the body requires them but can't make them from other food components.

Good fat is essential for us in many ways and EFAs are major nutrients. These essential fatty acids are required for the body's production of hormones and the smooth functioning of the brain and nervous system. EFAs also act as carriers for important fat-soluble vitamins A, D, E and K. In addition, dietary fats are needed for the conversion of carotene to vitamin A, for mineral absorption, and for a host of other biological processes.

Around 60 per cent of the weight of our brain, the fat-richest organ in our body, is fat and one-third of that is EFAs. Many studies have hypothesised that children who get enough EFAs can learn faster and focus better, and that there is a link between attention deficit disorder and a serious lack of EFAs. It is also thought that it is more likely that babies, children, adolescents and adults can become depressed when not getting enough EFAs.

What I'd like you to know as well is that EFAs protect us from dehydration because they help to form a barrier in our skin against loss of moisture. Thus EFAs also help prevent constipation and the toxicity that can result from it as, in a way, it lubricates the whole body from the inside out, at the same time making the skin soft, smooth and velvety beautiful. Dry skin indicates a need for EFAs. Skin is also said to tan better and burn less if the body is getting enough EFAs. They are also claimed to help with skin conditions such as eczema, acne and psoriasis. Consider this: we can live with dry skin but not with a dry brain or liver. Inner organs get priority on the EFAs brought into the body so only after the inner organs have had their share does the skin get oiled.

EFAs also make red blood cells more flexible, which means that they can find their way through capillaries more easily. The result of this is that cells and tissues receive their supply of nutrients and oxygen more effectively, which can greatly increase stamina.

I also want to point out that obviously we are not all the same and I do believe (without any evidence really) that people react in different ways, so some are able to handle a lack of nutrients like EFAs better than others; some are more delicate. But still I emphasise that it is relatively easy to make sure your baby gets enough of the right kind of fat, and I believe it is also very much worth it.

Note that it is much more difficult to get enough omega-3s in one's diet than omega-6, but extremely important, so I recommend taking an omega-3 rich oil always in the morning and I myself rotate hemp and flax seed with krill oil or purified fish oil in my home so my family and I get omega-3s most days from both the animal and plant kingdom. Omega-6 is much easier to obtain from one's diet.

I recommend buying only cold-pressed, preferably organic, oils in dark glass bottles. I keep mine in the fridge (except olive and coconut oil), use them mainly raw in my food after I have cooked it. Some, such as hemp oil and pumpkin seed oil, I simply take from a spoon, 1 tablespoon 3-4 times a week.

Omega-6 is found in the following foods:
Acai berries
Avocado
Blackcurrant seed oil
Evening primrose
Flax or linseed oil
Hemp oil
Almonds, nuts and seeds
Pumpkin seed oil
Safflower oil
Sunflower seed oil
Whole grains

Omega-3 is found in the following foods:
Acai
Chia seeds
Cold water oily fish (wild best)
Flax seed oil
Hemp seeds and oil
Krill oil and purified fish oil
Meat, milk, cheese, etc. from grass-fed organic cows contain more omega-3 than from non-organic cows, which are raised on grains or something even worse
Organic grass fed meat (and eggs)
Walnuts

Trans fatty acids

Unlike saturated, polyunsaturated and monounsaturated fats, trans fats or trans fatty acids are largely artificial fats (not good).

Trans fats are made by adding hydrogen atoms to unsaturated vegetable oils through a process called hydrogenation, which converts them into solid fat. Trans fats are thus more solid than vegetable oils, making them less likely to spoil. The purpose of hydrogenation is to increase the flavour, stability and shelf life of the processed foods in which they are used. They also have a very high melting point and can be re-used in deep-fat frying (very unhealthy!).

A small quantity of trans fats occurs naturally in meat and dairy products but it is the man-made trans fats in processed foods that are harmful.

To cut a long story short, trans fatty acids are extremely unhealthy for us and should be avoided at all costs. Research indicates that consumption of trans fatty acids increases our chances of heart and cardiovascular diseases, as well as type II diabetes and allergies.

When reading the ingredients list on products, it is sensible to steer clear of processed products containing hydrogenated fat and also partially hydrogenated fat. It is also best, as far as possible, to avoid foods that have been deep-fried, like French fries, chips, doughnuts and other buttery pastries. Exceptions do not matter.

The right kind of fats

Oils and good fats should be part of a healthy diet just like all other food, and it is important to remember that we do need fats in our diet, as long as they are the right fats. Those who are overweight are sometimes not eating enough good essential fats. As a result they develop food cravings and eat too much starchy and sweet food. They become carbohydrate junkies. The body turns all carbohydrates that are not burned for energy into fat. So eating less fat is making us fat! But it is the right kind of fat, the EFAs, that we need, not the processed trans fats. Protein and good fats stabilise blood sugar levels and leave you feeling fuller and more satisfied which, in turn takes away cravings for unhealthy processed foods.

Parents should definitely start eating cold-pressed organic oils and good essential fats. I put oils on my salad, often lemon-infused olive oil or pumpkin seed oil, but also check out my salad dressing on page 156. Furthermore, we use cold-pressed olive oil on our pasta, pizza, lasagne and on bread. I love it. I make my own garlic oil by pressing a fair amount of garlic into a glass jar and then I simply add olive oil – or other oils you like – and keep it in a sealed bottle in the fridge. I always put this on pasta. The oil lasts about three weeks, then I discard the garlic oil leftovers and make a new one.

> If you don't buy organic oils you should still always opt for cold-pressed extra virgin (raw) oils and I only buy oils in dark glass containers.

Giving your baby EFAs

I believe a healthy eating regime is one of the most valuable things you can introduce to your baby. From around 6 months of age, you can feed your baby organic cold-pressed hemp seed oil or flaxseed oil 1–2 tsp a day. I always give an omega-3 oil in the morning. It is very important to keep them in the fridge, as they are delicate oils and keep better when stored away from heat, light and air. When your baby starts eating two or three times a day, you can add more oils to the food. You could next use organic cold-pressed and unrefined (this is very important) olive oil, coconut oil, pumpkin seed oil and sunflower oil. I would put 1–2 tsp of organic raw unrefined oil into everything your baby eats. You can also sometimes use 2 tsp organic butter or cream. Always remember to put oils on your baby's food after you have cooked it because otherwise you are destroying the very essential nutrients you are aiming to provide. And as your baby is nearer to one year, you can start giving them krill oil or purified fish oil (around 1–2 tsp every day). You should always check your own baby's needs with your health visitor or doctor.

Salt

Your baby's kidneys are not fully developed until around the age of one. This means that a baby's kidneys do not have the capacity to rid their body of salt. It is therefore very important not to use salt before the age of one and to stay clear of salty foods. Many spice blends are heavily salted, so it is good to read the list of ingredients to make sure. And, of course, it is always best to buy pure spices. However, you don't have to avoid salt altogether; just use it sparingly, and I always use pure sea salt or Himalaya salt. Also, bear in mind that food which we might perceive to be flavourless might be full of flavour to a baby.

Fruits

Fruits are very easily digested and therefore do not give us long-lasting energy and a feeling of fullness. But don't get me wrong, they are still totally necessary in everyone's diet. I just want to emphasise that if you are feeding your baby pure fruit purée, your baby will probably become hungry again in an hour or so. I use fruits in between meals and sometimes also as a light breakfast (I like that myself very much together with my chia porridge) and also as something to nibble on at night before bedtime. When you add chia seeds, avocado, almond butter or sesame butter (tahini) to the fruit purée, it will give your baby more long-lasting energy because of the added protein and fat.

Sugar and sweeteners

Many have grown very tired of hearing about how we all are eating way too much sugar. But I am not sure many people realise just how much sugar we really are consuming. White sugar, or sucrose, is a highly refined product (= not good). Refined sugar is bad for us because it raises the insulin level in our blood. Raised blood insulin levels depress the immune system and if our immune system is depressed, then our ability to fight disease is weakened. Secondly, it can also cause weight gain when we eat to much of it. What's more, white, refined sugar contains no minerals or vitamins so in order for it to be metabolised it must use the body's reserve of vitamins and minerals, leaving us depleted.

Sugar is being added to all kinds of things – things you wouldn't and couldn't even imagine contained sugar, for example: bread, meat products, processed vegetables, peanut butter, mayonnaise and even some toothpaste. It really is a good idea to read the ingredients list before you buy.

High-fructose corn syrup

What is even worse (if possible) in my opinion is the high fructose corn syrup (HFCS), a highly refined and artificial product. It is created through an intricate process that transforms cornflour into a thick, clear liquid. This manufactured fructose is sweeter than sugar in an unhealthy way and is digested differently in a bad way. Research has shown that high-fructose corn syrup goes directly to the liver, releasing enzymes that instruct the body to store fat. This may elevate triglyceride (fat in blood) levels and elevate HDL cholesterol levels. This fake fructose may slow fat-burning and cause weight gain. Other research indicates that it does not stimulate insulin production, which usually creates a sense of being full. This means it can lead to people over eating, leading to weight gain. In the United States it has become very common in processed foods and beverages, including breads, cereals, breakfast bars, lunch meats, yoghurts, soups and condiments.

Sweeteners

Then there are artificial sweeteners. In short, I advise you to avoid them too, especially for your children.

When you start using bananas and other sweet fruits, dates and other dried fruits to sweeten your food, as well as organic palm sugar, honey, maple syrup, yacon syrup, agave nectar and others (always in moderation, of course), you'll soon see that you have no need for refined white sugar or high-fructose corn syrup. Also, if you make sure you are eating enough of essential fatty acids and good-quality proteins, you crave sugar and sweet things far less because they stabilise blood sugar levels and give you a feeling of fullness.

> It is always the same rule of thumb if you want you and your family and children to be healthy: avoid all processed foods as much as you can and eat a simple diet of fresh, natural foods. That is really all you need to know.

Preserving the Nutrients

Many nutrients are quite delicate and spoil easily if they come into contact with oxygen, water, heat and light, so the way you cook foods will impact on their nutritional value. You also need to store them correctly to maintain their good qualities.

The best ways to cook

That is why I recommend steaming vegetables – and fruits, too – when possible because that way they become more flavourful and are more nutritious than when boiled in water. If you do boil vegetables, keep the lid on. Steaming means that the vegetables are put into a steamer of some sort (the main feature is that it has holes in it!) and they sit there with water boiling underneath, so the steam cooks the vegetables but the water never touches them – and that's the trick! It is best to have the water boiling before you put the steamer with the vegetables on or into the pot. Keep an eye on the pan and top up with boiling water if the water is boiling away. Remember to cut the vegetables or fruits into similar-sized pieces because then they will all be ready at the same time. It is also good to stir or shake the vegetables half way through the cooking time for even steaming.

Cold-pressed unrefined organic coconut oil and grape seed oil seem to tolerate heat best of all the natural vegetable fats. It is also fine to sometimes use olive oil. Clarified butter or ghee is also a good option for frying at higher temperatures since its easy-to-burn milk solids have been removed.

Furthermore and very important: using a lower heat when cooking is much healthier for us. When making soups and stews, you can simply sauté the onions with the spices in a little water instead of oil. It is also possible to sauté in a small amount of water at a medium-low temperature and add a splash of your favourite oil near the end. The characteristic flavour of stir-frying will be retained without risking damage to the oil and, ultimately, to our health. Cold-pressed vegetable oils are very healthy for us but they are very sensitive to heat, light and air. They should mostly be consumed raw.

Preparing food

It is important to rinse all vegetables, fruits and salad ingredients properly before preparing them, especially if they are not organic (organic salads are often pre-rinsed). I only buy organic salads because it is very difficult to wash off anything that may have been sprayed on ordinary crops. I usually peel non-organic fruits and often vegetables. If you are buying from your local farmer (which is the best source) you can simply ask him how he grows his product and if he uses pesticides on his crop. Some do not, although they may not have taken the trouble to get organic certification.

Never let food like vegetables, salad and fruits come in contact with raw meat. Use cutting boards in different colours and never cut vegetables, salad and fruits on the same board as raw meat.

I do recommend good-quality steel or enamel pots or saucepans when cooking for your family and that you do not use Teflon material, which is supposedly toxic when heated. You may want to research this further.

Storing food

It is always best to cool food quickly to inhibit bacteria growth and mould. Transfer the food you want to keep to a ceramic or glass container, cover and put straight in the fridge, or pack appropriately in an airtight container, label and freeze. I highly recommend glass or ceramic containers for storing food. I myself keep clean glass jars with lids in my kitchen and use them for leftovers or for storing juice.

When you use jars for storing, make sure they are clean and sterile. Wash them thoroughly, and rinse them well in hot water. You could also pour boiling water in the jars to kill any bacteria that might still be lurking around, pour out the water again and let the jars air dry.

Freezing and thawing

It is very easy to freeze steamed, puréed vegetables in ice cube trays or small glass jars. I put a freezer bag over the ice cube trays and try to close it as tightly as possible. Often you can buy ice cube trays with a lid. Also if you have small glass jars, you can use the lid to close them well. If you are using ice cube trays you can take the frozen vegetable cubes out of the ice cube trays the next day and keep them in a well-sealed freezer bag or in a large glass or ceramic container. I have a permanent marker in my kitchen and I try to write dates on the bags when I put this and that in the freezer so that I know when it should be discarded.

When my children were babies I used to take one or two (or more) vegetable ice cubes out of the freezer before I went to bed and kept them in the fridge overnight to use the following day. If you forget to do that, you can also put your frozen vegetable cubes in a heatproof bowl and sit it over a pan of hot water until melted. It is also easy to put one or two frozen vegetable cubes into the pot in which you have just boiled some whole grains for your baby, as the frozen vegetable cubes will melt easily in the warm porridge but also cool it down to a nice temperature so your baby can start eating immediately. Don't forget to add a little cold-pressed oil, butter or cream to the meal before you serve it.

Don't forget:

- You should never refreeze food that has already been frozen. You have to eat it yourself or discard it.
- You should discard baby food that has been reheated once or, even better, eat the leftovers yourself.
- The safest way to thaw food is to do it overnight in the fridge, and not at room temperature.
- You must discard food that has come in contact with saliva, since the bacteria in the saliva will spoil the food very quickly.

Hygiene

Another important consideration is hygiene. When you are making food, it is extremely important to make sure that hands, tables, tablecloths, utensils and other kitchen appliances used are clean. And remember that you also have to change your washing up brush or sponge every now and then and/or put it in your dishwasher from time to time. You should always wash your hands before you start cooking, especially if you have just come home from shopping, for example. Just imagine all the people who have touched the same money and objects that you did. And not everybody washes their hands after they have used the toilet or sneezed. Washing your hands has proved to be one of the most efficient ways to stay clear of common colds and flu. Another advantage is that food keeps much better when you follow good hygiene rules.

Eco-friendly detergents are good for everybody, the environment and therefore nature's products (our food) and our skin. I highly recommend them. They also treat your clothes better!

It is good idea to change your tablecloths and napkins at least every other day. It is best to put them through a hot wash in your washing machine to kill all bacteria and mould. Most people use far too much detergent in their washing machines, which is not good for the environment, our skin or our washing machine. It is more than enough to use one tbsp or so. The same goes for dishwashers. And now it is possible to buy eco-friendly detergents, which I highly recommend. They will not harm your environment, your drinking water or the food that you are growing.

In my kitchen I always have one towel to dry eating and serving utensils and another one to dry my hands and a kitchen rug (in some lovely colours!) to keep all tables clean. I change all these three every other day and boil them in my washing machine to kill any bacteria. Wet, dirty towels are a good place for bacteria to blossom.

Cotton wipes for babies

The skin is our biggest organ. Everything we put on our skin seeps into our system, therefore we should only put on our skin things that would be safe to eat. (I admit, I have creams I do not fancy eating but you get the picture.) When it comes to babies I would take it very seriously. These unspoiled, pure little bodies, how can we not? It is very easy, for example, to use small cotton cloths when you are changing your baby's nappy. You simply wet them with warm water and maybe some organic oil like coconut or jojoba. Any smells are eliminated by the oil. And sometimes I also used a few drops of organic essential lavender oil. Lavender is soothing, relaxing, healing, anti-viral, anti-fungal and anti-bacterial. It is safe to use on babies. After using them, I used to put my cotton cloths in a basket that I had filled up with cold water and some sea salt or bicarbonate of soda (a couple of tbsp). After a few days, I simply fished them out of the bicarbonate of soda water with my hands and put them straight into the washing machine and then I boiled all of them. You can also use gauzes but you have to throw them away after each use. The cotton cloths are therefore friendlier and more sustainable to our environment.

Soap and shampoo

Regarding soap, babies are not dirty and do not need any soap and definitely not the regular ones with all kinds of unwanted and unnecessary chemical substances in them. I advise you to read the list of ingredients. It is enough to simply wash babies and children with warm water and a little oil and/or lavender. When I use lavender, I put a tsp of sea salt in my hand and a few drops of lavender oil into the salt and then put the salt into the bath. Sounds complicated but it is not. Sea salt is also a natural disinfectant. This is all you need.

My daughter used an organic shampoo for the first time when she was 7 years old. Until then I only put warm water, sea salt and lavender in her bath. I stopped using the oil when her hair became longer and it started to look greasy instead of clean after the bath! My son is now 7 and has never used soap. He smells delicious, I have to say; he has his own sweet smell. I put lavender in his hair and coconut oil (and sometimes Epsom salts) in his bath. Lovely!

We also have an internal cleaning system that I think we partly destroy with all this unnatural soap and artificial fragrances. I, myself, mostly use warm water and then I buy my shampoo, conditioner and other products in health stores. But I always read the list of ingredients and make sure they have no chemicals in them. I want them to be as 'clean' and natural as possible for me, my future water supplies and my environment in general.

I want to share with you that I take off my make up in the night with warm water, cotton pads and coconut oil. I love it. I also use coconut oil as a moisturising body lotion after bathing, as well as for my face. Oddly enough, it has inbuilt natural sun protection, and furthermore it is antifungal, antiviral and antibacterial. And last but not least, I use it as a deep conditioner for my hair every now and then. I wet my hair and damp it dry, put coconut oil in it and massage well. I then leave it for 30 minutes or more and then rinse and shampoo as usual.

Gathering your Ingredients

When I first started making food I was slow and made a lot of mess in the kitchen. All my focus and energy went into following the recipe and guidelines! But with time, practice and patience I became quick and neat so please do not give up! Practise makes perfect!

Here are some tips on buying quality fruit and vegetables:

- Vegetables loose nutrients over time so it is best to choose fresh ones from your store. You can also ask on what days new deliveries are brought into the store. And if you have a farmers' market in your vicinity or can buy from a local farmer, that is great. I would ask if pesticides are used.
- There is a lot of vitamin C in all green lettuce, parsley, red peppers, papayas, strawberries, kiwi, oranges, nectarines, lemons, passion fruit, gooseberries, goji berries, acai berries, tomatoes, mango and sweet potatoes, to name a few.
- Remember to only peel the part of the fruit you are going to use. Put the rest of the fruit with its peel in a closed bag/box/glass and keep in the fridge.

> The grape-like purple acai berry grows in Brazil's Amazonian rainforest. You can buy it freeze dried in powder form. It is a good source of antioxidants, essential amino acids and essential fatty acids.

Here are some general guidelines on how to buy, prepare and store some common fruits.

Apple

Some apples are sweet and some are sour and some in between. Apples do, though, become sweeter when kept at room temperature, although they do not have to ripen at room temperature. It is best to select sweeter varieties for small babies and/or keep them at room temperature for a few days. Apples keep for 2–4 weeks in the refrigerator.

- If you have a farmers' market in your area, you will probably find really good apples there. They are often more fresh than the commercial ones and may contain fewer pesticides … ask your farmer. If not, I'd go for organic varieties.
- I recommend organic or 'farming for the future' apples.

Avocado

I love avocado and so do all children I know who have been given it since they were young. I highly recommend avocado for young babies (and their parents for that matter!). It is an excellent first food. It has the essential fat that is so important to all of us, vitamin E and high-

quality protein. When babies have dry or hard stools, avocado comes to the rescue (as well as cold-pressed oils and chia seeds)!

Like any other fruit, the avocado has to be ripe before we eat it. If you buy it hard, it should sit at room temperature until it becomes a little softer. It ripens faster if it is sitting next to a banana (not kidding!). When the narrower end becomes soft and the avocado yields to gentle pressure, it is ripe and ready to be eaten. When it is ripe, but you are not going to use it right away, move it to the fridge where it will keep for a week or so.

When ripe and you are ready to eat it, a knife will slide through the flesh to cut it in half, so you can gently twist the halves off the stone, then the green avocado flesh is easily spooned out. If it has a tiny spot of brown flesh, just cut it away and discard it (if the avocado is all brown or black, just throw it away). Also, if it never ripens and becomes soft so it is not possible to spoon out the flesh, I throw it away as well.

When babies first start eating, they are only able to eat very little, so there is no way you would give them a whole avocado. What you can do in that case is to store the half with the stone in it in a closed container and it will keep in the fridge for up to 24 hours. Lemon or lime juice (for babies older than one year) also acts as a preservative as well as being a wonderful 'spice' or flavour enhancer in food!

Avocado is also great in salads, with Mexican food and any food really. Simply spoon out the flesh, cut it into bits and squeeze a little lemon or lime juice over it.

Banana

Bananas ripen at room temperature like any other fruit and become sweeter and more easily digested by our bodies. When a banana is ripe you can put it in the fridge for a week or so where the ripening process almost stops.

You can also freeze ripe bananas. I first peel them, cut them in half and then I freeze them in a freezer bag or other container. Babies who are teething often like being served something cold that soothes their sore gums, and a piece of frozen banana is ideal to make a purée very cold.

Ripe fruits are much healthier for us than unripe (more alkalising, for example, which is very positive for our bodies). They also taste much better; usually sweeter, softer and juicier.

Mango

The mango needs to ripen at room temperature until it is soft and yields to gentle pressure. Then you keep it in the fridge after that to halt the ripening process, as with almost every other fruit.

When you are cutting a ripe mango, it should be sweet, soft, very juicy and beautifully yellow. Ripe mango puréed with a ripe pear, for instance, and a pinch of vanilla powder and a hint of rice or almond milk tastes like heaven. I also love mangos in my salad.

Cucumbers are actually a fruit and cucumber and mango salsa (along with some red onions, lime juice, ginger, olive oil and fresh herbs) tastes great with any food and is very refreshing. Cucumbers are suitable for babies over 8 months. Dried mango is also a great candy for children who can chew well, and the same goes for dried apples.

Papaya

Papaya is a wonderful fruit for small babies. I love it as a light breakfast. It is full of vitamin C and also digestive enzymes, which are essential for good digestion and can thus help with bowel movements and prevent constipation.

It is best to buy a ripe papaya by selecting a fruit that is predominantly yellow. If you cannot find a ripe papaya, a green unripe papaya can be placed in a paper bag for a few days to facilitate ripening. Often the skin of the papaya will begin to wrinkle a bit when ripe but it does not affect the quality or flavour of the fruit. Soft brown/greenish spots, on the other hand, indicate it is spoiled. A ripe papaya should have a light, sweet smell. If it is unripe, it will have very little smell at all and overripe will have an overpowering sweet smell. If you are not about to use the ripe papaya right away, I suggest you keep it in the refrigerator in a plastic bag to halt the ripening process. I do not recommend freezing papaya as it partly destroys the texture and flavour of the fruit.

Young children love fruits. But they need help for many years to be able to eat them. They need to be washed, sometimes peeled, then cut into suitable pieces. It is our responsibility to serve our kids fruits (instead of biscuits, chips, sugary yoghurts and cereals) and the same goes for vegetables (which are great cut into strips) and most other healthy food for that matter!

Pear

Like all fruits, pears are much sweeter, juicier and softer when ripe. If you buy a pear that is not ripe, keep it at room temperature for a few days or until it becomes softer and yields to a gentle pressure. After that you keep it in the fridge where it keeps for at least four days. Be careful with ripe pears as they are very delicate and bruise easily.

Pineapple

I recommend picking a nice golden-coloured pineapple, all the way around the fruit. It is still good and ripe even though it has green on the upper portion. A dark brown (greyish) colour means it is overripe or spoiled. You can also smell the bottom side for a fresh, sweet aroma. If the aroma is only faint, it might not be ripening as it should. Pineapples are always sweeter toward the bottom of the fruit and therefore I always give my kids those slices. It becomes more sour towards the top. A ripe pineapple keeps in the fridge for a couple of days.

When puréeing food for your baby the quantity of liquid you need may vary. Soft fruits for example need very little liquid. Always start with just a little and gradually add more until you reach the consistency you think suits your baby. As your baby grows older it is a good idea to mash or finely cut the food instead of puréeing to practise chewing.

Let's Start Making Baby Food!

These are simple purées to make for your baby when you start weaning. In these first recipes, I don't necessarily say exactly how much water, juice or fruit to use when you are puréeing because you need to make the purée just right for your baby. The amount of liquid depends on how you want your purée – thick or thin – so start with the fruit and just add the liquid gradually until you have the consistency you want. You will soon know how much of each ingredient you will need to include and, in any event, you will need to change that as your baby's needs quickly change. Good luck with everything and don't be scared or intimidated – if something goes 'wrong', just mark it up to experience – do not give up, it is part of the learning process. Last but not least, this is all much easier and more fun than you think, I promise you! And your reward is a happy, healthy baby.

- Start by washing the fruit or vegetables and drying on a clean cloth.
- Peel, stone or core the fruit or veg, as appropriate, then cut into similar-sized pieces.
- Cook gently with a little liquid, as outlined in the recipes, then blend to a purée, adding liquid as necessary.
- It tastes good to add a pinch of organic pure vanilla powder into purées as well as cinnamon.
- It is also lovely to purée sometimes with organic coconut water, carrot or apple juice, organic almond milk or rice milk at the appropriate time for your baby. The possibilities are endless!
- Baby food does not need added sugar. When you are making baby fruit purées and you think they are not sweet enough, you can always add a little ripe banana or a date, for example.

I usually use organic pure vanilla powder (bourbon vanilla), which you can buy in delicatessens selling organic products or online (including from Amazon). You could also use organic vanilla bean paste (available from Waitrose) or split a vanilla pod and scrape out the seeds. Vanilla extract often includes alcohol so read the label and only use a pure product.

Apple

Take two apples, rinse them well, dry and peel them. Cut them into pieces and steam them, or boil in a little water, for about 4 minutes. Purée with a little water, breast milk, organic formula or organic coconut water, and later maybe a little pure organic carrot juice.

When your child reaches 7 months, there is no need to boil or steam the apples any more and you can also skip it if the apples are sweet and purée well for a small mouth.

Apple purée keeps for around 1–2 days in the fridge and 2 months in the freezer. However, I recommend making new apple purée as you go along, as it does not take a lot of time to peel an apple and purée with a little liquid.

- I only peel non-organic apples and apples for small babies who have just started eating.
- It is a nice variation to purée the apples with a pinch of ground cinnamon or vanilla powder for one baby portion.
- It is also good to keep some soaked organic dates in the fridge in a glass jar (or apricots, prunes or similar fruits) to put 1–2 into the purée from time to time. Prunes help prevent constipation and are a good source of iron, as are dried apricots.
- Make sure the dried fruit you buy has not been handled with the preservative sulphur dioxide.
- All whole, raw food contains protein, whether it is a vegetable, fruit, seed or a nut.

Vegetable purées keep in the fridge for about 2 days and in the freezer for around 2 months. Fruit purées keep in the fridge for about 1–2 days and in the freezer for around 2 months. However, I always recommend making new fruit purées each day for your baby since they are quick and easy to prepare and do not require any cooking time. I think fresh is best and older siblings, mum or dad can enjoy the leftovers.

Avocado

Wash the avocado and slice it through, but be careful, there is a big stone in the middle, which you discard (just squeeze it out!) and then spoon out the flesh. To begin with, you can purée the avocado with breast milk, formula, water, coconut water or organic carrot juice.

Later you could also add a pear, an apple, steamed carrot, banana or whatever. It takes on the flavour of the other fruit since the avocado does not have a strong flavour by itself. I very often purée it with an apple in some water and maybe a little pure organic juice with a pinch of vanilla powder and put some superfoods in it to make my Green Baby Purée (see page 125). It is my green super yoghurt! Puréed avocado only keeps for around 12–24 hours in the fridge.

Banana

Pick a small, very ripe banana. Peel the banana and simply purée it with a little water. You can also use breast milk, organic formula, pure organic coconut water, organic rice milk, organic carrot juice and so on. A little added vanilla is also nice. Eat straight away!
Older babies often find it extremely fun and tasty to dip a banana into a bowl of desiccated coconut – which may also keep them preoccupied for a while!

Carrot

First I'd like to tell you that I highly recommend organic carrots or 'farming for the future' carrots since carrots absorb substances from the surrounding soil so well. It is therefore very important that the ground they are grown in is clean and healthy! This, of course, applies to all foods; some maintain that malnutrition starts in the soil.

Take a few carrots, rinse them well and peel if they are still dirty or if you find any ugly spots you dislike on them. Cut them into even-sized pieces; the size of the pieces determines the cooking time. If they are cut into bite-size pieces it should not take more than 10 minutes to boil or steam them. They are ready when you can stick a fork quite lightly through them. Then purée them using some of the water they were steamed or boiled in to thin the purée for a small baby. I use my hand-held blender and a Pyrex measuring jug for small portions or and my food processor for bigger portions. The purée keeps for around 3 days in the fridge and for 2 months in the freezer.

- It is very important to add organic cold-pressed unrefined oil or organic butter or cream to the carrot purée so your baby can better utilise the vitamin A, which is naturally found in carrots and is a fat-soluble vitamin. Vitamins D, E and K are also fat-soluble. Always remember to put oils into your baby's food after you have cooked it. They are most nutritious and beneficial raw but can become harmful if overheated (fried). I do not put oils or fats into food that I am going to freeze; I only ever put it in immediately before feeding.

- Clean small glass jars with a lid come in handy to use for the purée in the fridge. They are see-through and they do not give any unwanted substances back into your baby's food.

Usually the cooking time is made longer for small babies in order make it easier to purée their food very smoothly, but as they grow older it is wise to cut down on the cooking time a little to preserve the delicate vitamin C and to keep the vegetables more crisp.

Mango

When mango is in season, it makes a delicious purée. Simply wash it and dry with a clean cloth. Peel it and cut out the flesh towards the stone in the middle. Discard the stone. Purée it with a little water or the tiniest drop of organic coconut water – you hardly need any – and serve! It keeps in the fridge for around 1–2 days and in the freezer for about 2 months. You can also freeze ripe mango chunks to use in purées or smoothies! What I also love is ripe mango pieces sprinkled with a little desiccated coconut – a delicious dessert!

Millet

Millet is naturally gluten-free and a lovely grain to introduce to a baby. If the millet is finely milled, all you have to do is put it in a sieve and rinse it with cold water or, even better, hot boiled water as well. Then you pop it in a pan with 2 parts water for every 1 part millet (but 1½ portions if pre-soaked) and boil it for 2 minutes or so. If you are using whole millet, it is best if you soak it for an hour or two (or overnight) in cold water and then rinse it under cold running water, again in a sieve. Then put it in a pan with fresh water, in the same ratio as the milled millet, and boil it gently for around 10–20 minutes (20 minutes if not soaked and 10 if pre-soaked). Then you can purée it for your baby with some extra liquid and cooked vegetables. Remember to put 1–2 tsp cold-pressed oil (from a dark glass bottle) into your baby's purée at the end. Cooked millet can keep in the fridge for about 3 days.

Quinoa

I recommend quinoa as one of baby's first foods after 6 months. If the quinoa is finely milled (like baby porridge), all you have to do is put it it in a sieve and rinse with cold water or, even better, if you use hot boiled water as well. You then boil it for 2 minutes or so (1 portion quinoa and 2 portions water or 1½ portions water if pre-soaked, see below). If you are using whole quinoa, you need to soak it for an hour or two (or overnight) in cold water and then rinse it under cold running water, again in a sieve, and then put it in a pan with fresh water and boil it for around 10–20 minutes (20 minutes if not soaked and 10 if pre-soaked). Then you can purée it for your baby with some extra liquid and cooked vegetables. Remember to put 1–2 tsp cold-pressed oil (from a dark glass bottle) or organic butter or cream into your baby's purée at the end.

You can keep cooked quinoa in the fridge in a glass jar with a lid for about 3 days. I myself love my quinoa with cold-pressed lemon olive oil and ripe mango bits or apple bits. It is too good to be true! See the recipe on page 139.

> Bear in mind that your baby is not used to what you are used to, which means that your baby might enjoy foods you personally don't like or you might consider tasteless: not sweet or salty enough, too plain, and so on. So keep an open mind, use fresh, quality ingredients, keep foods plain (don't mix too many foods, which also makes life easier for you), put some tender love and care into the cooking and everything will turn out great!

What is quinoa?

Quinoa (pronounced keen-wah) is an ancient food that has been cultivated in the South American Andes since at least 3,000 BC and has been a staple food for millions of native inhabitants. The ancient Incas called quinoa the 'mother grain' and revered it as sacred.

Technically quinoa is not a true grain, but the seeds of the Goosefoot plant. It is used as a grain and substituted for grains because of its cooking charactcristics. The size of the quinoa seed is somewhere between a sesame seed and millet.

Quinoa has a delightful, unique characteristic: as it cooks, the outer germ around each grain twists outward forming a little white, spiral tail, which is attached to the kernel. The grain itself is soft and delicate and the tail is crunchy, which creates an interesting texture combination and pleasant 'crunch' when eating the grain. Quinoa has a fluffy consistency and a mild, delicate, slightly nutty flavour.

The seeds must be rinsed before cooking to remove the bitter resin-like coating, which is called saponin. I recommend an overnight soak, or at least 1–2 hours, then rinsing it under cold running water in a sieve before boiling it. The seeds cook in only 10 minutes. If you don't have time, you could also rinse it with hot boiled water in a sieve, in which case you need to cook it for 15–20 minutes.

The quinoa seed is high in protein, calcium and iron, a relatively good source of vitamin E and several of the B vitamins. It contains an almost perfect balance of all eight essential amino acids needed for tissue development in humans. It is exceptionally high in lysine, cystine and methionine-amino acids typically low in other grains. It is a good complement for vegetables, which are often low in methionine and cystine. The 12–18 per cent protein in quinoa is considered to be a complete protein due to the presence of all eight essential amino acids. The 6–7 per cent fat content in quinoa is relatively high when compared to other grains. The quinoa seeds are gluten-free, which makes it a nutritious alternative grain for those with gluten sensitivity.

Due to the relatively high oil and fat content of quinoa, the grains and flour should be stored in the refrigerator or in a relatively cool place.

Papaya

Rinse the papaya and dry it with a clean cloth. Cut it in half and spoon out the small seeds. Peel both of the halves and purée them with very little water. You won't need much additional liquid to purée them well for a small baby since it is a very soft fruit (if it is not soft, it is not ripe). This purée keeps in the fridge for 1–2 days.

There is no need to give your baby fruit juices to drink in the first year because they could take away important space in your baby's tummy from the breast milk/formula or healthy food. But after one year, it is fine for a treat but then you should definitely dilute it one portion of juice with four to five portions of water, which also saves money. When children grow older, you can very easily make your own popsicles by freezing diluted pure organic fruit juices. All children love that.

Pear and Peach

Wash a ripe pear or a peach (or both) well and dry with a clean cloth or paper. Peel and remove the stone. Put the pear/peach in a small pan with a little water (2-4 tbsp) and simply boil it over a low heat for 1 minute or so. Puree it, for instance, with a handheld blender in a Pyrex glass jug or similar. You can also steam the pear/peach. The puree keeps in the fridge for 1-2 days and about 2 months in the freezer, but it's always best to make it fresh as you need it. When your baby is 6 months old you don't have to boil/steam the pear/peach, but always use ripe fruit as it's much sweeter, softer and healthier!

Pumpkin

Wash your pumpkin and peel it with a knife. Be careful not to cut yourself. I would cut it in half first and then put both halves down on your cutting board and cut the peel downwards. Spoon out the seeds in the middle and cut the pumpkin in bite-size chunks, preferably all the same size. Then you simply boil or steam it for around 10–15 minutes and purée it with some of the cooking water as well as some cold-pressed oil or organic butter or cream. You can easily freeze the purée in ice cube trays. This keeps in the fridge for around 2 days and in the freezer for about 2 months.
• You can purée 2–3 apples with the pumpkin, which gives it a very nice flavour. Cinnamon also complements the flavour of the pumpkin.

Sweet potato

Wash one sweet potato well, dry with a clean kitchen paper, then peel using a potato peeler or a sharp knife. Cut the potato into chunks and try to make them all just about the same size. It takes longer to cook bigger pieces. Preferably steam (or boil) the sweet potato for about 10–15 minutes, but again, it depends on how big the pieces are. The sweet potato is ready when you can easily put a knife or fork through the pieces. Then you simply purée the potato with some of the water used to steam it (boil it). You could, of course, mash it with a fork but sometimes there are long threads in the potato, which can be a choking hazard for small babies.

You can freeze the purée in ice cube trays or small glass jars. If you use an ice cube tray it is good to put a freezer bag over it and close it well before it is put in the freezer. Sweet potato purée keeps in the fridge for 2–3 days and in the freezer for about 2 months. Remember to write on the bag or jar when you made it.

- Of course you can also boil vegetables in water. Then you simply cut the vegetables, put them in a pot with water just about covering them, and boil with the lid on until soft. Then you purée the cooked vegetables with some of the boiling water. Start with a little water and keep adding until the purée has reached the desired consistency. You can also bake a whole sweet potato for an hour at 180°C/Gas 4. When ready, the peel will come off easily and you can purée it with some water and organic butter or olive oil.
- If your child has started eating porridge, it is nice to mix it with sweet potato purée and, a little later, with some cold-pressed extra virgin organic oil, butter or cream.
- Remember to add healthy fats (cold-pressed oils) to the meal after you have cooked the food, since cold-pressed oils are very sensitive to heat, light and oxygen and are best consumed raw.

Recipes for Babies from 6 Months

If you have started with the basic purées, then gradually you will want to introduce more flavours to your baby's diet. Do so gradually, one at a time. Remember that there are some things that you simply don't like, so your baby is entitled to the same likes and dislikes! Stay with one flavour at a time until you think your baby is ready for a bit more variety.

Some children do not want their food mixed up! They like their grains separate (their porridge) from their fruit purée as well as their vegetable purée. So if you are having trouble feeding your child porridge with fruit purée or vegetable purée, try to give these separately as it might just do the trick for your baby, but always remember to add the cold-pressed organic oil (or butter or cream). All kids love that, guaranteed.

While we are talking about food preparation, I would like to reiterate that I do not recommend using a microwave when cooking for babies, or for anyone for that matter! I have heard so many stories where parents stop warming or cooking food for their babies in the microwave and suddenly their babies start eating vegetable purées and all the rest and, better yet, start loving it. I like to believe that children have an intrinsic unspoiled taste for nature, meaning a taste for fresh, living foods. I also believe that microwaves kill our food, stripping it of nutrients, which to me means that it cannot give us life and energy. Anyway, give it a go if you have a fussy eater in your home. And last but not least, remember to feed your baby when he or she is hungry, that is, has not eaten for at least 2 hours. Everything tastes better when you are hungry. Good luck!

I haven't given specific portion quantities for the recipes as every baby will be different. Instead, I have followed the common sense approach and given logical quantities based on the ingredients.

Remember:
- Wash and dry fresh fruits and vegetables before you start.
- Always use ripe fruit and fresh vegetables.

- I like to use organic produce.
- Refer to the lists on pages 26–30 to check whether additional ingredients are suitable for your baby's age.

Homemade carrot juice

It is amazing I tell you! It is very easy to make your own carrot juice! Simply buy organic or 'farming for the future' carrots, wash them (peel only if necessary), cut into chunks and put them through your juicer! Then, if your child is 12 months or more, squeeze just a little fresh lemon juice into the carrot juice to gives it extra vitamin C, enhance the sweet flavour of the carrots and make it last longer in the fridge. Go for it! Just keep it in a clean glass bottle in your fridge where it should keep for 3 days. If you do not use any lemon, it will last only around 1–2 days in the fridge.

- I love juicing 6 carrots and 1 apple with a little lemon juice!
- I also love juicing 6 carrots, 1 apple, 1cm piece of root ginger and a stick of celery with a little lemon juice.
- You can freeze your carrot and apple juice in lollipop moulds as a treat!

Avocado and carrot juice

1 avocado
Organic carrot juice (bought or homemade) to thin down to the desired consistency

- Halve the avocado, remove and discard the stone, then spoon out the flesh.
- Purée it with the carrot juice.

Banana, pear and carrot juice

1 banana
1 pear
Water and/or organic carrot juice

- Peel the banana, and peel and core the pear.
- Purée together with the carrot juice, making it as thick or thin you like.

- If it is too thin you can always teach your baby to drink it with a straw!
- If you don't have a banana, just purée two ripe pears together with the carrot juice … my, oh my, it tastes delicious!
- Optionally you can add a pinch of vanilla powder, if you wish.

Apple, pear and banana

½ banana
½ apple
½ pear
Liquid of your choice: water, breast milk, organic formula, organic coconut water, organic carrot juice, organic apple juice, etc.

- Peel the banana, and peel and core the apple and pear.
- Purée the flesh all together with a liquid of your choosing.
- Eat immediately.

- I recommend that mum or dad finish the rest, but it keeps in the fridge for a day or so. Alternatively, you could freeze this in a lollipop mould for older siblings.
- You can also use avocado instead of pear, or peach if your baby is over 7 months.
- You are doing your baby a world of good if you make it grow accustomed to drinking water at meal times and in between meals.
- If you buy fruit juices for your baby's purées it is smart to buy either organic or make sure they do not contain anything else except the fruit juice – no additives, sweeteners, colours or other additions.

> I do not recommend that you freeze a puréed avocado or banana because it turns brown when it is thawed and becomes less tasteful, although it is fine if you intend to eat it partly frozen like an ice-cream!

Avocado and pear

1 avocado
1 pear
1 tbsp organic cold-pressed coconut oil
Extra water, if necessary

- Halve the avocado, remove and discard the stone (squeeze it out) and spoon out the flesh. Peel and core the pear.
- Purée everything together with the coconut oil and added water, if needed.

- A little ripe papaya would be lovely in this one too. Mum and dad can eat the leftovers!

Papaya, pear, banana and mango

½ papaya
½ banana
½ mango
1 pear (optional)
½ tsp vanilla powder
Water or organic coconut water
Organic rice milk to thin down to the desired consistency (you can use almond milk after 9 months)

◆ Peel all the fruits, and stone or core them.
◆ Purée the flesh with the vanilla and water or milk. Eat straight away.

● You can also use rice milk instead of water if your baby is 7 months, or almond milk if your baby is 9 months old. Another alternative is is to use pure organic carrot juice.
● Older siblings or mum and dad can enjoy the leftovers!
● You can always freeze leftover fruit purées in lollipop moulds for older family members to enjoy as an ice-cream.
● If some of the food in the baby's fruit purée is frozen, the purée will become cold. Babies who are teething sometimes like that a lot since it cools their sore gums.

Sweet potato with cinnamon

1 sweet potato
Cooking water to thin down to the desired consistency
¼ tsp ground cinnamon

◆ Peel the sweet potato and chop it into bite-size chunks.
◆ Steam or boil it for about 10–15 minutes, depending on the size of the pieces.
◆ Purée with a little of the water used to steam or boil it, and the cinnamon.

• This keeps in the fridge for about 2 days and you can also freeze it in ice cube trays for about 2 months.

• Remember to put a little cold-pressed oil, cream or butter in the meal for your baby – around 2 tsp.

If your child does not want to eat the purée you made for them, please do not be upset or disappointed. (I've been there and I did both! I do not recommend it, it does not help matters and there is no fun in it!) Try to allow your child instead to read a little book or draw a picture and the little mouth might open and forget to be fussy. If nothing works, just eat it yourself and try this specific taste again in one or two weeks. Sometimes it takes a while to get used to some flavours and we all have different tastes. But with resilience and patience we can get used to pretty much anything. Some say that when a child does not like a specific taste, it might take up to eight attempts for the child to grow accustomed to it. Some babies also love to feed on their own and are more willing to try new foods that way. Last but not least your baby needs to be hungry. Hunger is the best spice ever!

Recipes for Babies from 7 Months

Once your baby is 7 months old, you will be able to introduce more foods to their diet. Take a look at the list on page 28 and introduce new flavours only one at a time.

Remember:
- Quantities are based on convenience of making the purées so may make one portion or more, depending on your baby.
- Wash and dry fresh fruits and vegetables before you start.
- Always use ripe fruit and fresh vegetables.
- I like to use organic produce.
- Refer to the lists on pages 26–30 to check whether additional ingredients are suitable for your baby's age.

Apple and avocado with mango juice

1 apple
1 avocado
½ tsp vanilla powder
1 tsp organic white tahini (optional)
Water or organic coconut water and/or organic mango or pear juice to thin down to the desired consistency

- ◆ Peel and core the apple. Cut the avocado in half, discard the stone and spoon out the flesh.
- ◆ Purée the apple and the avocado with the vanilla, tahini, water and juice. Enjoy immediately.

- Mum and dad can enjoy any leftovers or it will keep in the fridge for a day or so.
- You can add ½ tsp organic spirulina if you like once your baby is 12 months old.
- Fruit purées without a banana or avocado will keep for 1–2 days in the fridge but fruit purées with a banana or avocado only keep for around 12–24 hours in the fridge.

Apple and banana

1 apple
1 banana
Water, organic coconut water or carrot juice to thin down to the desired
  consistency

◆ Halve, peel and core the apple, then chop it in even-sized
  pieces. Peel the banana.
◆ Purée the two together with a little water, coconut water or
  organic carrot juice instead of water.

Apple and carrots

2 carrots
1 apple
1–2 tbsp goji berries (optional)
Water to thin down to the desired consistency

◆ Peel the carrots, if necessary. Peel and core the apple and cut
  them both into even-sized pieces.
◆ Steam or boil the carrots until they become soft when you poke
  them with a fork. The time it takes for them to become ready
  depends upon the size of the pieces, but about 10 minutes.
◆ Purée them with the apple and the goji berries with a little of
  the water you cooked the carrots in. You can also add a little
  organic apple juice, if you prefer.

• This keeps in the fridge for around 2 days and in the freezer for
  about 2 months.
• It is nice to mix this with a little porridge made with quinoa,
  buckwheat, millet or oats.
• Also, remember to put a little cold-pressed oil in the meal for
  your baby (around 2 tsp).

What are goji berries? Goji berries, also known as Chinese wolfberries, are renowned
in Asia as one of nature's most nutrient-rich foods. Goji berries have been used in
traditional Chinese medicine for over 1,700 years. They are a true superfood that
everybody can enjoy. To name a few benefits, they contain 18 amino acids, the
building blocks of protein, including all eight that are essential for life. They contain
21 trace minerals, including germanium, an anti-cancer trace mineral rarely found in
foods. They contain more carotene than carrots and high levels of vitamin C, as well
as vitamins E and B-complex. Goji berries are also a source of essential fatty acids and
solavetivone, a powerful anti-fungal and anti-bacterial compound. And the list goes
on. I often throw them into my shake. You can add them to just about any purée for
your child when you feel like it.

Apple porridge with cinnamon and vanilla

About 80g prepared porridge such as rice, quinoa, millet or oats
1 apple
1–2 tbsp blueberries, fresh or frozen
¼ tsp ground cinnamon
¼ tsp vanilla powder
2 tbsp apple or other juice
Organic rice milk to thin down to the desired consistency

- Make the porridge as you usually would.
- When it is ready, purée it together with all the remaining ingredients.

- You can use almond milk and/or almond butter in the purees once your baby is over 9 months old.

Dried apricot, apple and pear

4 dried sulphur-free apricots
2 apples
1 pear
Water to thin down to the desired consistency

- Pre-soak the apricots for an hour or so to make them soft enough to purée well. If you don't have time, just chop them. Wash the apples and the pear and peel and core them.
- Purée everything together with some water.

- You can keep this in your fridge for around 2 days and in the freezer for 2 months.
- This purée is great with a little organic yoghurt or Greek yoghurt.
- You could also make it with dried figs.

Avocado, pear and blueberry

1 avocado
1 pear
¼ banana
1 tbsp blueberries
Water to thin down to the desired consistency

◆ Halve the avocado, remove and discard the stone and spoon out the flesh. Peel and core the pear. Peel the banana.
◆ Purée the avocado and the pear along with the banana, blueberries and water.

● After 9 months, you could use organic almond milk instead of water, or 1 tsp organic pure almond butter and water instead of the almond milk.

Broccoli

1 head of broccoli

◆ Cut the broccoli into even-sized pieces.
◆ Bring a pan of water to the boil and begin by boiling or steaming the tough stalks for about 5 minutes, then add the flower heads and keep on steaming or boiling for another 5 minutes or so, depending on the size of the pieces.
◆ Then you simply purée the broccoli with a little of the water that was used for the cooking.

● Organic butter and a little sea salt go well with the broccoli flavour, as does cold-pressed olive oil.
● Remember to add oils when all the cooking has been completed, so as not to destroy the essential nutrients of the oil you really want to benefit from.
● For older members of the family, broccoli goes really well with almost any food and is abundant in nutrients. I recommend that you put the chopped broccoli into boiling water and count to 10 and then take it out and serve warm with sea salt and, if you

like, pure butter or olive oil. When you do this you manage to rinse the broccoli and make it soft and warm, without destroying any of its good nutrients.

Broccoli and potato

300g broccoli florets
2 medium-sized potatoes
6 basil leaves (optional)
Unsalted organic butter or olive oil
A pinch of sea salt
Water to thin down to the desired consistency

◆ Steam the broccoli for around 10 minutes. Boil the potatoes in water for about 20 minutes, depending on their size. When cooked, drain and peel the potatoes.
◆ Purée the potatoes and broccoli with the basil, if like, butter or olive oil, sea salt and water. Be careful not to purée this for too long otherwise the potatoes will become chewy! If your baby has started chewing, it is ideal to mash the potatoes with a fork and then blend it manually with the broccoli purée.

Herbs like basil and parsley keep well in a glass jar in the freezer to put into vegetable purées when needed. And you can freeze the vegetable purée even though you have pre-frozen herbs in it!

Date purée

This is very easy! I soak fresh, stoned dates overnight in a glass container with a little water (let the water almost cover them but not quite). And then you can throw this in your food processor or blender and purée to a desired consistency. Put it in a glass jar or plastic container (BPA free!) and keep it in the freezer This date purée never freezes entirely, so you can always take a little to sweeten your porridge, your yoghurt or anything else you might need it for.

Mango and avocado

½ mango
½ avocado
½ tsp vanilla powder (optional)
1 tsp cold-pressed coconut oil
Water or organic coconut water to thin down to the desired consistency

◆ Peel half the mango and avocado.
◆ Purée with a little vanilla powder and water or coconut water.

• This is an amazing combo.
• Leave the stones in the unpeeled halves of the mango and avocado, and store in the fridge, preferably in a sealed container. Use within 24 hours or so.
• After your baby is 8 months, you could add 1 tbsp chia seeds or 1tsp white tahini.
• You could also add some pure organic mango juice or other favourite juice.

Mango and pear with organic rice milk and vanilla

½ mango
½ banana
1 pear
1 tsp vanilla powder
Organic rice milk to thin down to the desired consistency
Organic Bourbon vanilla (powder) to garnish (optional)

◆ Peel the mango and banana, and peel and core the pear.
◆ Purée everything together with rice milk.

• After your baby is 8 months, you could add 1 tbsp chia seeds.
• After your baby is 9 months, you could use almond milk instead of rice milk, or 1 tbsp organic pure almond butter and water.

Parsnip and turnip

1 parsnip
1 turnip

◆ Peel the parsnip and turnip, then cut it into bite-size chunks, preferably all the same size.
◆ Steam or boil the vegetables for about 10–15 minutes or until soft, then purée with some of the water used to cook them.

• This keeps in the fridge for about 2 days and in the freezer for about 2 months.
• Remember to add organic cold-pressed vegetable oil to the purée or organic butter or cream when you serve.
• Parsnips and turnips go well with vegetables like carrots, sweet potatoes, potatoes, broccoli and cauliflower.

Peach, apple and pear

1 peach
1 apple
1 pear
1 tsp organic white tahini
⅓ tsp vanilla powder (optional)
Water or organic carrot juice to thin down to the desired consistency

◆ Peel and stone the peach, and peel and core the apple and pear.
◆ Purée with the tahini, vanilla powder and water or carrot juice.

Pear and peach

1 pear
1 peach
2–4 tbsp water

◆ Peel and stone the pear and peach and cut into even-sized pieces.
◆ Put the fruit in a small pan with a little water and simply boil over a low heat for 1 minute or so until soft. Alternatively you can steam the pear or peach if you prefer.
◆ Purée it in a blender or with a hand-held blender in a glass jug.

• This keeps in the fridge for 1–2 days and about 2 months in the freezer. However, I recommend making new purée as you go along, since it takes little time and fresh is always best.
• It is much easier to purée 2–3 pears or peaches at a time.
• If your baby is over 7 months, it is not essential to cook the pear or peach. Just make sure you use ripe ones for your baby (they are much sweeter, softer and healthier!), peel it and purée with a little water to a smooth consistency. You won't need much liquid since ripe pear is a soft fruit.
• It is also very nice to steam or boil this combination with a fresh date or dried apricot, especially if you have a few softened in the fridge (see page 104), in which case they purée very easily. You simply take out as many dates/apricots as you like and you can also use some of the sweet water they were soaked in for the purée.
• This would go well with a little organic Greek yoghurt.

Sweet potato and broccoli

1 small sweet potato
100g broccoli
1 tbsp unsalted organic butter
About 120ml breast milk, organic formula, organic rice milk or organic milk

◆ Peel the sweet potato and cut it and the broccoli into bite-sized chunks.
◆ Steam the sweet potato for about 10–15 minutes, depending on the size of the chunks.
◆ Steam the broccoli as well for about 10–15 minutes and remember to steam the tough stalks for around 5 minutes longer.
◆ Purée everything with the butter, adding more if necessary, and the milk.
● You can also just use water.

Finger Food

Giving your child finger foods to eat allows them to practise their manual dexterity and co-ordination. Babies can usually start eating finger foods around 7–9 months old. It varies between children when they are ready. Parents need only make sure that they are never alone when eating finger foods and make necessary arrangements so that food does not get stuck in their throat. They cannot eat in the car! To begin with, the bites are made very small – the size of a raisin.

Gradually parents will learn what kind of food their child manages to eat, chew and swallow. But it is always sensible not to give them too much at once since they tend to stuff their mouth with too much food, which could raise the risk of something getting stuck in their throat.

Super finger food
- Small pieces of ripe avocado.
- Well-ripe fruit, washed, peeled and cut into very small pieces.
- Cooked soft vegetables, cut into small pieces.
- Peeled courgette, cut into very small bites.
- Organic dried cranberries (good if soaked for at least an hour in water).
- Organic goji berries (good if soaked for at least an hour in water).
- Organic stoned prunes (good if soaked for at least an hour in water), cut into small pieces.
- Organic stoned dates (good if soaked for at least an hour in water), cut into small pieces.
- Organic dried apricots (good if soaked for at least an hour in water), cut into small pieces.
- Organic raisins, in moderation and definitely organic (good if soaked for at least an hour in water).
- Cooked sweetcorn (preferably organic)
- Cooked brown rice (preferably organic).
- Hard-boiled yolks (preferably organic) (or eggs after your baby is

one year old) cut into small pieces.

- Whole grain bread without coarse grains (such as spelt/kamut, gluten-free or sprouted), cut into pieces. You can put organic butter on the bread, or olive oil. You can also let the bread pieces float in a bowl of water, organic milk, almond milk or rice milk (depending on the age of your baby) and let your baby fish them out.
- Organic spelt/kamut pasta or gluten-free pasta cooked well and cut into small pieces.
- Cooked beans (I rinse them first in a sieve if I buy them ready and I recommend buying them in glass jars and not tin cans).
- You can buy a very safe food feeder net for your baby so they can nibble on foods without the choking hazard. Check it out!

Soaked dried fruits are softer and contain less condensed sugar since they have been rehydrated.

Recipes for Babies from 8 Months

Now your baby is likely to be getting much more adventurous so you can begin to introduce more fruits, like fresh apricots, some fresh herbs, fish and cucumber.

Remember:

- Quantities are based on convenience of making the purées so may make one portion or more, depending on your baby.
- Wash and dry fresh fruits and vegetables before you start.
- Always use ripe fruit and fresh vegetables.
- I like to use organic produce.
- Refer to the lists on pages 26–30 to check whether additional ingredients are suitable for your baby's age.

Chia porridge

This is easy, fast, raw and super healthy!

3 tbsp chia seeds
200ml water

- ◆ Blend the seeds and water together in a bowl and leave to stand for around 10 minutes, stirring occasionally, until the chia seeds have absorbed the water and the mixture starts to resemble a porridge.

Chia seeds

Chia seeds are wonderful. Chia seeds are one of the greatest plant sources of a omega-3 fatty acid called alpha linoleic acid or ALA. The soluble fibre in the seeds soothe the digestive system and slows the release of sugars into the blood stream, stabilising blood sugar levels. The antioxidants naturally preserve the delicate omega-3 oils and provide an anti-ageing benefit as well. They are also a fine source of calcium, zinc and iron. And for sports people everywhere, the combination of fibre, fats and protein make chia seeds an excellent food for fitness and endurance. I love them because they make me feel so good. It is easier to keep your ideal weight when

you make chia seeds a part of your diet since they bulk up meals with low-calorie nutrient density and their taste is very mild and pleasant. Chia seeds are a great travel food, too. They can also help with constipation.

For your baby, you can always purée 1–2 tbsp chia seeds with their fruit or vegetable purée, as well as mix them into their porridge.

For me, I use them in my shakes (around 2 tbsp) and I also love eating my chia seeds as a porridge with a little cinnamon and fruits (ripe mango pieces are a favourite). It is also lovely to mix chia seeds with almond milk or almond chocolate milk (even hemp milk, which you make using the same recipe as almond milk, on page 102) for a chia almond or chocolate pudding. And then you can always add the fruits you like as well. I love goji berries and cacao nibbs in my chia porridge.

Apple and date

This is another recipe that makes it a good idea to have a few dates stored in a glass jar of water in the fridge, ready to be used in purées. This softens them so they blend very easily. Also use some of the water because that is very sweet too.

1–2 apples
2 dates, soaked in water for at least 1 hour
2 tbsp chia seeds (optional)
Water to thin down to the desired consistency
Pinch of ground cinnamon or a pinch of vanilla powder (optional)

◆ Peel, core and chop the apples. Chop the dates.
◆ Purée the apples with the chopped dates and the chia seeds with a little water.
◆ You can also add a little ground cinnamon or vanilla if you like.

• This keeps for 2 days in the fridge and 2 months in the freezer.
• This would go well with a little organic Greek yoghurt, for example.

Mango and apple

½ ripe mango
1 apple or pear
1 tbsp goji berries
1 tsp organic tahini
Water to thin down to the desired consistency

- Peel and stone the mango, and peel, core and chop the apple or pear.
- Purée the mango, apple, goji berries and tahini with some water. You can also use almond milk or organic rice milk instead of water.

- Do not peel the other half of the mango if you are not using it right away and keep it in the fridge.
- If you find the purée to be not sweet enough you can always add a little banana or 1 date.
- If your child is over 9 months, you can add 1 tsp organic pure almond butter.
- Remember you can always add a little vanilla, cinnamon etc. to give that extra sweet yummy flavour to baby purées or your smoothie. And if you add avocado the texture will be very creamy!

Sometimes kids are eager to eat some particular food for a while and then one day, just like magic, they don't seem to like it any more. Don't worry about this – it is very normal. Everybody grows tired of food if they eat it too often. Just try something new; this is a great time to do so. It is also good to bear in mind that we increase the chances of sensitivity or intolerance to certain foods when we eat the same food day in and day out without any breaks. Rotation is the key to a wholesome and diverse diet.

Prune with apple and peach

Make sure you buy prunes that have not been treated with sulphur dioxide.

1 apple
1 peach
2–4 prunes, stoned, pre-soaked in a little water if possible
Water or organic apple juice to thin down to the desired consistency

♦ Peel, core and chop the apple, peel and stone the peach. Chop the prunes.
♦ Purée everything together with some water, or organic apple juice, just a little, also tastes lovely in this one.

• This keeps in the fridge for about 2 days or in the freezer for 2 months.

• I recommend adding 1 tbsp chia seeds in this puree, as well as 1 tsp white tahini, for some essential fats and protein.

Before they are a year old, liquids other than breast milk and organic formula can take precious space away from healthy foods in your baby's tummy. I always recommend teaching babies to from early on to drink water in between meals and with meals and nothing else. Just plain fresh water. At 6 months it is natural and normal that your baby starts drinking less and less breast milk or organic formula and taking in more food and water. But this happens slowly from the age of 6 months to a year. But milk (organic milk, almond milk, rice milk, coconut milk, and so on) can be used and mixed in smoothies, baby food and in cooking. But in a glass for babies and children water is best.

Prune and banana

Prunes are a natural laxative (so they can prevent constipation), thanks to their rich fibre content, and they are a wonderful storehouse of antioxidants and beta-carotene. Prunes are furthermore a natural source of vitamin B6, copper and potassium. They give you a long-lasting and healthy energy boost. Make sure you buy sulphur-free prunes.

2–3 prunes, stoned
1 banana

◆ Water to thin down to the desired consistency.
◆ Soak the prunes in a little water for about 1 hour or more (unless you keep a few in the fridge in a glass jar in some water to use whenever you need them, soft and ready for any purée or smoothie). Peel the banana.
◆ Purée the prunes with the water they were soaked in along with the banana and simply add more water if needed. Eat right away.

● Mum and dad can finish the leftovers (if there are any!).
● Add an avocado, peeled and stoned, if you like!

Diets that contain fibre-rich foods, such as fruits and vegetables, and are low in fat, saturated fat and cholesterol, are linked to a reduced risk of heart disease and certain cancers.

Recipes for Babies from 9 Months

At 9 months old, you will be beginning to get closer to feeding your baby a similar diet to your own. Remember that their systems are still immature, though, so take it slow and steady.

Remember:

- Quantities are based on convenience of making the purées so may make one portion or more, depending on your baby.
- Wash and dry fresh fruits and vegetables before you start.
- Always use ripe fruit and fresh vegetables.
- I like to use organic produce.
- Refer to the lists on pages 26–30 to check whether additional ingredients are suitable for your baby's age.

> Once your baby reaches 9 months you can sometimes use almond milk for your baby's fruit purées – it is a nutritious option, so very nourishing and tastes absolutely wonderful. You can always throw in a ripe avocado, when you feel like it, to make the purée even creamier. You can also throw in a handful of organic salad leaves if you have some and purée with the rest. You can easily freeze leftover fruit purées in lollipop moulds for older children to enjoy as an ice-cream.

Homemade almond milk

It is very easy, honestly! See my how-to video on www.puréebba.com
same recipe as the almond milk seed and nut milks

150g almonds
3 dates, stoned
750ml water
Pinch of vanilla powder

- Put the almonds in a bowl and cover well with water. Leave to soak for 10–20 hours or overnight at room temperature.
- Rinse the almonds in clean water in a colander, discarding the soaking water.
- Put the almonds in your blender with the dates, vanilla and

750ml of fresh water and blend at high speed for a little while.

◆ Once you have blended it, you can obviously drink it as it is but for small children I would sieve it. This is how to do it. You use a milk nut bag (or a clean nylon sock!) and a big bowl. You pour the milk into the bag with the bowl under it. Then you place one hand (clean hands!) at the top of the bag for a firm and secure hold. With your other hand, squeeze the mass to allow it to release the 'milk' through the bag. When you have finished 'milking' your nut bag, you are pretty much left with the almond peel in the bag and the white silk-like milk in the bowl. You could also use a fine strainer.

◆ Now you only have to pour the milk into a clean glass bottle and keep it in the fridge. It keeps for about 2 days. Always taste it yourself before you feed it to your baby. You have to shake the milk before each use since it divides over time (into water and almonds), which is normal.

● I love adding to this recipe 1–2 tbsp goji berries.
● Once your baby is one, you can use 1 tbsp organic raw honey, agave nectar or yacon syrup instead of the dates if you prefer.
● Do not feed honey to infants under 12 months of age.
● You can also simply peel the almonds once they've been soaked, before you make the milk. It is quite easy and then you can skip the sieving process and just drink the milk as is. It's completely up to you, but small children often want it sieved.
● With this same recipe you can make hemp seed milk, sesame seed milk, pumpkin seed milk, macadamia nut milk, and so on. Just replace the almonds with whatever nuts or seeds you want to use. Children can have nuts after the first year and seeds after 8 months. I never use peanuts.

You can use the leftover pulp in your cakes!

When your baby is around 8–9 months old, you can also start soaking almonds overnight in cold, fresh water or for around 12–24 hours, changing the water they are soaked in after 10 hours to keep it fresh. Then you can always throw in a few of the soaked almonds when you are puréeing fruits for your baby. I peel them first, which should be easy once they have been soaked. After 12–24 hours, put fresh water on the almonds and keep them in a glass jar in your fridge. They should be consumed within 2–3 days and I would put fresh water on them every 24 hours.

Dried apricots with ripe pears and almond butter

I recommend that you keep a few organic non-sulphur-treated dried apricots in a little water in a glass jar with a lid in your fridge so they are soft and ready when you need to use them for purées.

2 dried apricots
1 pear
1 tsp organic pure almond butter or white tahini (optional)
About 80g prepared porridge like rice, quinoa, millet or oats, for
  example
Organic rice milk and pear juice (or other juice you like, and the juice
  is optional) to thin down to the desired consistency

◆ Chop the apricots finely if they are not pre-soaked. Peel, core and chop the pear.
◆ Purée the apricots, pear, almond butter, pear juice and organic rice milk with the porridge and serve immediately.

● Parents can enjoy the rest if there are any leftovers.
● How much pear juice and organic rice milk you use just depends on how thick or thin you want to make this. Just start with very little and add more.

Almonds are so greatly nourishing and, in short, a wonderful food for anyone who wants to be happy and healthy in their lifetime! Almonds are rich in monounsaturated fat, which helps you feel fuller for longer, and their high fibre content helps to keep blood sugar levels steady and prevent hunger pangs, therefore they are a great weight-loss choice. They are loaded with nutrients and contain a lot of calcium, iron, protein, magnesium and other nutrients. My life is better since I started eating almonds, nuts and seeds. Give it a go, it is not as difficult as you think!

Carrot and apple

¼ yellow onion or 1 leek (optional)
4 carrots
2 apples
½ tsp ground ginger
½ tbsp yeast and MSG-free vegetable stock or ½ cube
250ml water
Pinch of sea salt (optional)

◆ Peel the onion and carrots, if necessary, and cut into bite-size chunks. Peel, core and chop the apples.
◆ Put the fruit and vegetables into a small saucepan or pot with the remaining ingredients and boil for about 15 minutes over a low heat.
◆ Purée with a hand-held blender in the saucepan. Add a pinch of sea salt if needed.

• This keeps in the fridge for 2 days and in the freezer for 2 months.
• You can easily make the recipe bigger and serve it for the whole family.

Some children do not like it when foods are mixed together. In other words they want to eat apple purée with nothing else and their carrot purée with nothing else. That is just fine. They may, for instance, have a more delicate digestive system. Simple foods are more easily digested and strain the digestive system less.

Courgette

Courgette is such a nice vegetable. It doesn't have a strong flavour itself but takes on the flavours of those vegetables cooked and puréed with it. It gives a very nice texture to purées. I would steam it or boil it to begin with, just for a few minutes since it is so soft. But later on you should simply use it raw in your baby's purées. Raw food is very good for all of us as no nutrients or enzymes (essential for healthy digestion) have been spoiled through cooking. I would opt for organic varieties when possible!

Courgette and sweet potato

½ onion
½ sweet potato (or butternut squash)
½ courgette
½ tbsp yeast and MSG-free vegetable stock or ½ cube
250ml water
Pinch of sea salt (optional)

◆ Peel and chop the onion and sweet potato. Chop the courgette.
◆ Put everything in a relatively small saucepan or pot and boil over low heat for about 15 minutes.
◆ Purée everything using a hand-held blender. Add a pinch of sea salt if needed.

• This keeps in the fridge for around 2 days and in the freezer for about 2 months.

It is a good idea to try and have something very green with your dinner whenever possible. From green vegetables we get protein, vitamin C and calcium, just to name a few of the nutrients they contain. Also, vitamin C enhances iron absorption! Having said that, I want to tell you that you can buy, for instance, organic pure hemp seed powder or spirulina powder and from 6 months, I sometimes added just a little bit (around ½ tsp of the spirulina and 1 tsp of the hemp seeds) into my baby's fruit or vegetable purée.

Pear and blueberry with almond butter

1 pear
2 tbsp fresh or frozen organic blueberries
⅓ banana
1 tbsp organic pure almond butter, soaked almonds or white tahini
⅓ tsp ground cinnamon
Water to thin down to the desired consistency

◆ Peel, core and chop, although you may prefer to leave the skin on if the pear is organic and if your baby has not just started eating solids. Peel and chop the banana.
◆ Purée the pear with everything else in the recipe, starting with just a little cold water and adding until you reach the consistency you think suits your baby. If it becomes too thin (like a shake) you can always teach your baby to drink it with a straw!

Sweet potato and bean

½ leek
1 small sweet potato or butternut squash or little of both
250ml water
50g well-cooked organic beans (any beans you like)
1 tbsp unsalted organic butter

◆ Chop the leek. Peel and chop the sweet potato or squash.
◆ Simmer the leek and the sweet potato or squash in the water for 15 minutes over a low heat.
◆ Then remove from the heat, add the beans and the butter and purée everything with a hand-held blender, adding some more water if needed.

Recipes for Babies from 12 Months

I believe passionately in giving babies the best start in life by feeding them a healthy diet of fresh, organic, living, natural foods. I also try to serve food grown locally and in its due season for the best flavour and nutritional values.

Remember:
- Quantities are based on convenience of making the purées so may make one portion or more, depending on your baby.
- Wash and dry fresh fruits and vegetables before you start.
- Always use ripe fruit and fresh vegetables.
- I like to use organic produce.
- Refer to the lists on pages 26–30 to check whether additional ingredients are suitable for your baby's age.

Be creative in the kitchen!

Goji berry, banana and organic strawberry

If you can get your hands on coconut water for this recipe, that is great, but ordinary water will work just as well. I recommend organic strawberries or ones you know are not sprayed, which is unfortunately too often the case with strawberries and definitely not good for little bodies!

1 tbsp goji berries
1½ bananas
1 handful of organic strawberries
1 tbsp organic pure almond butter, soaked almonds or white tahini
Water or organic coconut water to thin down to the desired consistency

- ◆ If you like, soak the goji berries in a little water overnight to make them soft, although this is not necessary.
- ◆ Peel the banana. Purée the goji berries and the soaking water with the banana and strawberries, adding a little more water if necessary.

• You can also add 1 tsp of organic raw coconut oil to this purée as well as 1 tsp vanilla powder.

Lentils with cauliflower purée

1 leek (optional)
1 carrot
⅓–½ cauliflower
1–2 handfuls of kale (optional)
60g red or yellow lentils
400–500ml water
1 tbsp yeast and MSG-free vegetable stock or 1 cube

◆ Chop the leek, carrot and cauliflower into bite-size chunks.
  Chop the kale.
◆ Put everything together in a relatively small saucepan or pot and
  boil over low heat for about 20 minutes.
◆ Purée in the pan with a hand-held blender.

● This keeps in the fridge for 2 days and freezer for 2 months.

> Red lentils are a nice alternative to meat in a meal. They are high in protein and iron
> and do not need to be soaked before cooking. But if you do have the time and energy,
> they become more easily digested when soaked. Furthermore, they are cheap and give
> a nice flavour to soups and stews. I especially like them in the cold winter.

● Remember to add some organic cold-pressed oil like hemp,
  pumpkin, olive or coconut oil to your baby's vegetable purées,
  since vegetables are naturally very low in fat. Babies need fat
  even more than we do. It is essential for them.
● It is also nice to blend a little baby porridge with a vegetable
  purée. Your child will feel fuller longer than when only eating
  steamed carrots, for example.

> Vegetable purées go well with fish and meat purées when children are old enough to have
> those (see my lists on pages 26–30). I always recommend organic meat. Those who do
> not want to give their children meat do not have to worry, though, because a varied
> vegetarian diet with plenty of raw fruits, vegetables, leafy greens, super greens like
> spirulina powder or wheatgrass powder, whole grains, pulses, beans, raw (preferably
> soaked) almonds, nuts and seeds provides everything we need to be healthy and happy.

Raspberry

When in season, I recommend organic or 'farming for the future' raspberries.

1 pear
1 small banana
2–3 tbsp organic fresh or frozen raspberries
1 tsp organic white tahini
1 tbsp goji berries (optional)
½ tsp vanilla powder or ground cinnamon (optional)
Water to thin down to the desired consistency

◆ Peel and core the pear and peel the banana.
◆ Then simply purée everything together well, starting with very little water and adding until you reach the consistency you think suits your baby. Add some more banana if you think it is too sour.

• You can always add an avocado for that extra creamy texture.
• You can do the same thing with organic strawberries as well as other berries, when in season, for children over one year old.

Pineapple

The pineapple is sweeter towards the bottom and more sour at the top. I would purée the sweeter part for a small baby and eat the more sour part myself. It is great before dinner to help with digestion, like when you are cooking and very hungry! Pineapple is loaded with enzymes for your digestion, just like the papaya.

2 slices pineapple
1 banana
Water to thin down to the desired consistency

◆ Cut away the skin and the core of the pineapple. Peel the banana.
◆ Simply purée the fruits with a little water until you reach the desired consistency.

● If your baby is 9 months, then you can use almond milk instead of water.
● This will keep for 2 days in the fridge and 2 months in the freezer.
● I also often add 1 tbsp of organic almond butter or cream and 1–2 tbsp of desiccated coconut.

Healthy Shakes for Everybody

Now your baby is one year old – where has the time gone?! Now they are really part of the family inn terms of what they are eating. The recipes in this chapter make around two servings.

Fruit and vegetable juices

Before one year of age it is unnecessary to give a child fruit juices to drink. It could actually take up precious space from nutritious food or breast milk. However, you can sometimes use pure fruit juices (preferably organic or that you juice yourself) when you are making fruit purées for your baby. I advise you to always read the ingredients when buying fruit juice to make sure that it contains only 100 per cent juice and preferably not from concentrate. After one year of age you can sometimes give your child fruit juice to drink but I would always dilute it one part juice and four to five parts water. It is not healthy for a little child to drink maybe the equivalent of 5–10 apples or oranges from juice in just a few minutes.

Vegetable juices are all great. If you have your own juicer I would definitely try juicing organic carrots. I have not yet heard of or met a baby who doesn't like carrot juice. Or you can buy organic carrot juice; you can use it for the purées and also, after the age of one, to drink. But to begin with I would also dilute the carrot juice around one portion carrot juice and two portions water. My son is now 7 years old and he still wants a glass of carrot juice a day. Sometimes I mix into it 1 tsp acidophilus in powder form for him.

Juices and shakes

The juices and shakes in this chapter taste wonderful for everybody in the family to enjoy. They are also very easy to make, honestly!
- Shakes can serve as a light, nutritious breakfast for the whole family but can also provide a good energy boost later in the day or even serve as a light dinner.
- If you usc almonds (for babies older than 9 months) or cashews

(for babies older than 1 year) or seeds (for babies older than 8 months), you will add to your family's diet the essential fat we all need in order to stay happy and healthy, good proteins and essential minerals like calcium, magnesium, zinc, iron and more.

- The first rule is that there are no rules! Just throw in what you have got and you like – if you make sure you always have plenty of seasonal fresh fruits and veggies at home, you are in good shape! And remember, if you think you will not be able to eat all you have purchased, just wash, peel, cut and freeze it in a BPA-free container.
- I always soak almonds, nuts and seeds in glass containers.
- I freeze ripe bananas (peeled and cut in half) to use in my shakes but you can always use a little less water and put some ice into your shakes instead to make them cold. Not all blenders can blend frozen bananas but if you defrost them for about 10–15 minutes before blending it usually works well.
- Some like their shakes thin, others thick! Always start with less water and gradually add more until you reach the desired consistency. Soon you will start using your judgement instead of measurement tools to know how much you need!

Embrace the exercise and enjoy your food! We don't need to spend hours in the gym to stay in shape. And you don't even need the gym for that matter. I want to tell you what has worked for me. I exercise for around 20–30 minutes, three times a week. I exercise really hard for around 30 seconds so I am completely out of breath after that time. And then you exercise slower for around 90 seconds and repeat this process about eight times. Then it is good to stretch a bit and sometimes I have time to do some muscle exercises as well – just a few. This kind of exercise makes one burn many more calories and for a longer period of time, or long after you stop. I love this and recommend it wholeheartedly. But everything counts, of course, and therefore it is good to try to incorporate exercise as well into your daily regime. Take the stairs, walk to the store, do a few push ups while your soup is cooking. Something (even just a little) is always better than nothing!

Fruit and vegetable health shake

This makes a lovely meal in a glass. Try it with frozen bananas, which makes the shake cold. The vanilla powder or cinnamon makes it sweeter.

1–2 bananas
1 small apple, 3 lychees or ½ mango (depending on what is in season)
1–2 dates, prunes, dried cranberries, figs or other dried fruit you like
1 handful of berries, pineapple or other ripe sweet sour fruit (depending on what is in season)
2 handfuls of organic green salad
A pinch of vanilla powder or ground cinnamon (optional)
½ avocado
Water or organic coconut water, depending on how thick or thin you want to have it

♦ Peel the bananas. Core the apples, or peel and stone the lychees, or peel and stone the mango.
♦ Blend everything except the avocado together and then add the avocado last and blend for a little while longer.

• You can also add some pre-soaked seeds, nuts or almonds into this one, around 1–2 tbsp.
• Sometimes I add 1 tsp organic tahini for calcium, essential fat and protein.
• Often I put 1–2 tbsp organic cold-pressed coconut oil or hemp oil into my shakes.
• And last but not least, you can put some nice superfood powder in it like spirulina, yacon powder, baobab, cacao powder, hemp seed powder, acai powder or other.
• If there are leftovers you can put them in a glass jar with a lid and keep for 12–24 hours in the fridge.
• You can also freeze this as an ice-cream. You can also make healthy ice treats by freezing diluted pure organic juice in lollipop moulds. You can even freeze only water; it is amazing how much children like that!

Now as you can see this is not difficult. All you need is good will and the belief that this will do you and your family a world of good. You are eating an unbelievably raw, nutritious food (raw meaning that no nutrients have been destroyed through cooking). Your body will thank you.

My Hanna's shake

40g almonds
1 frozen banana (it will make the shake cold)
½ tsp vanilla powder
200–250ml organic rice milk, water or organic coconut water

◆ Soak the almonds overnight in water.
◆ Drain and rinse your almonds and I would recommend that you peel them. It is easy once they have been soaked as they simply slip out of the skins.
◆ Then you simply put all the ingredients in a high-speed blender and blend until smooth, then enjoy immediately!

Blueberry almond shake with pear

50g almonds or cashews
150g fresh or frozen blueberries (or other berries you like and are in
  season)
1 frozen banana (it will make the shake cold)
1–2 dates, stoned
1 ripe pear (optional)
200–250ml water or organic coconut water

◆ Soak the almonds or cashews overnight in water.
◆ Drain and rinse your almonds or cashews. If you use almonds, I
  would recommend that you peel them. It is easy once they have
  been soaked as the skins just slide off.
◆ Then you simply put all the ingredients in a high-speed blender
  and blend until smooth, and enjoy immediately!

• Optionally, throw in ½ avocado.
• I also love to add ½ chopped mango.

And if you need more protein, after a workout, for example, I
recommend organic pure whey protein. One scoop of that and
these shakes start to resemble an ice-cream.

Blueberry almond shake with goji berries

250ml almond milk
100g frozen blueberries
1 banana
2 tbsp goji berries (optional)
1 tbsp cold-pressed coconut oil (optional)

◆ Throw everything into your blender and blend until smooth.
  Enjoy!

Strawberry and mango almond milk

Use organic strawberries if you can.

50g almonds
50g fresh or frozen strawberries
½ fresh or frozen mango
1 banana
2 dates, stoned and soaked, if liked
250ml water or organic coconut water

◆ Soak the almonds overnight in water.
◆ Rinse the almonds and discard the water they were soaked in, and I like to peel them.
◆ Throw everything in your blender, mix well, adding more water if you want to have it thinner. Enjoy immediately!

● I often add a pinch of vanilla powder.
● Optionally add 1 tbsp of organic raw cacao.
● If you do not like banana in your shakes, you can always substitute 3 dates or 1–2 tbsp organic honey, agave nectar or yacon syrup. That way you can also keep leftovers in your fridge for 1–2 days. If you use a banana, I find it only keeps in the fridge for 12–24 hours.

Happy goji shake

You will fall in love with this delicious shake! If the fruit is not frozen you can use some ice to make the shake cold.

50g almonds or cashews
1–2 tbsp goji berries
1 frozen banana
½ fresh or frozen mango
1–2 dates, stoned and soaked, if liked
250ml water or organic coconut water
1 tbsp cold-pressed raw coconut oil (optional)

◆ Soak the almonds overnight in water. You can soak the goji berries in a little water if you like to soften them.
◆ Rinse the almonds or cashews (if you are using almonds I would also peel them) in cold fresh water and discard the water they were soaked in.
◆ Throw everything in your blender, including the goji berry soaking water. Blend and enjoy.

• Sometimes I throw some superfoods like 1 tsp maca into this shake. I also like chia seeds (1–2 tbsp), yacon powder (1 tsp) and baobab powder (1 tsp) as well as organic pure whey protein (1 tbsp) after exercise.

Cacao beans are the seeds of the cacao fruit, which is a nut that grows on a jungle tree.

The cacao beans are 100 per cent pure dark chocolate. Raw cacao is an amazing superfood. It is a great food source of the heart-supporting magnesium and a great source of neurotransmitters, which help alleviate depression and are associated with feelings of well being. This makes cacao a natural anti-depressant. Eating raw cacao is also known to diminish the appetite and can therefore help people loose weight. Cacao beans also contain 10g per 100g of flavonol antioxidants, which makes cacao one of the richest sources of antioxidants of any food.

Antioxidants protect us from free radical damage of the skin. Essentially the darker the colour of the food, the more antioxidants it contains.

Chocolate almond milk

This will keep in your fridge for around 3 days.

60g almonds or cashews
2 tbsp organic cacao powder (raw is even better)
6–7 dates, stoned and soaked, if you like (or I use 4 dates and 3 drops
*   of chocolate stevia)*
½ tsp vanilla powder (optional)
500ml water

◆ Soak the almonds or cashews overnight in water.
◆ Rinse your almonds or cashews and discard the water they were soaked in.
◆ Blend everything together and sieve through a nut milk bag (see page 21).

● If I peel my almonds I don't sieve this drink and if I use cashews I do not sieve it either.
● Drinking sieved nut and seed milks strains your digestive system less, so it is a good option if you have a delicate digestion or if you are battling an illness. Kids often like it better that way as well.

Chocolate almond milk with banana

40g almonds, cashews or macadamia nuts
1 tbsp organic cacao powder (raw is even better)
1 frozen banana
Pinch of vanilla powder
250ml water
1 tbsp organic cold-pressed raw coconut oil (optional)

- ◆ Soak the almonds overnight in water.
- ◆ Rinse your nuts and discard the water they were soaked in. If you use almonds I would peel them. It is very easy once they have been soaked.
- ◆ Then you simply blend everything thoroughly together and enjoy immediately!

It is very easy to hide all kinds of green superfoods, for example, spirulina or blue green algae, in the flavour of the cacao. Both are so abundant in nutrients, you wouldn't believe it. For small babies I advise you to use just a little amount (½ tsp).

Quick and easy chocolate milk

This is perfect for when a sweet craving creeps up on you! I like to use a frozen banana to make the shake cold but you can use an ordinary one and add some ice.

1 frozen banana
1 tbsp organic cacao powder (raw is even better)
½ tsp vanilla powder or even a little ground cinnamon (both optional)
1 tbsp cold-pressed raw coconut oil (optional)
200ml water or organic coconut water (or even almond or coconut milk)

◆ Blend everything together and enjoy immediately!

• Tahini or organic pure almond butter, if you have any, would both be great in this one (1–2 tsp) for taste and added nutritients.
• You can also use ice instead of some of the water to make the shake cold and in that case the banana doesn't need to be frozen!
• I also like using carob powder sometimes instead of the cacao powder but watch out it does not taste like cacao!

Hemp seeds contain all the 10 essential amino acids, the building blocks of protein, or 30 per cent pure digestible protein, providing readily available amino acids for building and repairing tissue. Hemp seeds also contain all the essential fatty acids and are therefore considered to be a complete food. Furthermore they contain a wide array of nutrients, antioxidants and fibre. The fibre in hemp seeds is excellent for maintaining digestive and colon health. I love the nutty flavour of the hemp seeds and powder and use it often in my smoothies, the seeds in my quinoa porridge and I always buy raw and organic. You can easily add 1 tsp of it to your baby's purée every now and then from 9 months. Hemp seed is usually very safe for those unable to tolerate nuts. To avoid misunderstanding, hemp seeds do NOT contain THC.

Green baby purée

This is my green super yoghurt! I love it myself dearly. As you can see, you can make this very simple dish when in a hurry and you can make it into a superfood when you feel like it!

1 avocado
1 apple
1 tsp organic white tahini (optional)
Pinch of vanilla powder
1 tsp hemp seed powder or seeds (optional)
½ tsp organic pure spirulina (optional)
A few organic salad leaves (optional)
Pure organic coconut water
Pineapple juice or apple or pear juice

◆ Halve and stone the avocado, then scoop out the flesh. If you are making this super yoghurt for a very small baby, I would peel the apple; do so either way if the apple is not organic. I only leave the peel on when it is for older babies and the apple is organic.
◆ Then you simply purée all the ingredients into the desired consistency. I use my Pyrex jar and hand-held blender and I love mine like a thick yoghurt.

• Sometimes I use almond milk instead of water but then I skip the tahini.

Raw and living foods are uncooked fruits, vegetables, nuts, seeds and sprouted grains that are never heated above 42°C/118°F so as not to destroy their nutritional value or enzymes. Enzymes assist in the digestion of food and some say they are the life force of food. These raw foods can be eaten whole or combined to make the healthiest, most delicious meals. I try to eat a lot of raw foods myself because they make me feel good and happy!

For the Whole Family

I am going to start this chapter off with yummy vegetable soups which are all very easy to make and thus take almost no time in the kitchen. Served with healthy homemade bread, they will be enjoyed by the whole family. I hope you try them – you will not be disappointed. And for those dads who think they will not get full just by eating a vegetable soup, you are so wrong! They give you a light and pleasant fullness and lots of energy. I also sometimes serve my soups with a salad for my husband and myself to enjoy (and force feed my children a few leaves!). I promise you that only my favourite ones are here for you to enjoy! I love the spelt pan bread and naan bread on pages 196 and 199 with my vegetable soups.

I use water to heat (fry) the onions with the spices in my recipes. That is because oil always becomes unhealthy for us when fried. Unsaturated vegetable oils are sensitive to heat, which is why you should always buy cold-pressed oils in dark glass bottles, keep them in the fridge and use them mostly raw. Coconut oil, when you really need it, I think is by far the best choice for frying and sautéing and sometimes I use a little butter (you can also use ghee if you can get your hands on that) along with some water. You can also use olive oil. I just make sure I keep the heat on low and simply heat the onions with the spices until fragrant and soft. I also make popcorn out of coconut oil but I never use the highest temperature. It takes just a little while longer, a few minutes maybe, but you'll get a great tasting and rather healthy popcorn for everybody to enjoy!

> Cooking doesn't always have to be as accurate as many people think. Be creative in the kitchen! Be daring! It's fun to use your imagination in the kitchen.

MSG

I highly recommend that those of you who have not converted to MSG-free vegetable broth or stock do so now. If you read the ingredients on many store-bought broths and stock you will find that many of them contain MSG or mono-sodium glutamate, also referred to as 'the third spice', and I have seen it also labelled as 'MSG, permitted flavouring'! MSG is something that brings out flavour in food and it also makes food tender (so imagine what it does to us). It is not a natural food source; you can't grow the herb MSG in your garden! I think it is safe to say that very many people suffer from MSG intolerance, which includes symptoms such as headache, diarrhoea, stomach cramps, dizziness, uncontrollable thirst and so on and so forth. Unfortunately you can find MSG in many commercial stocks, packed and canned food, many processed meat products, even chips, and in all kinds of ready-made food products.

The good news is that nowadays you can buy vegetable stock and broth that contains no MSG or other artificial flavours or additives. They are usually organic as well. I also prefer vegetable broth and stock that are yeast-free. Yeast does not do us any good if we eat too much of it, which is very often the case since yeast is found in most bread products and many ready-made spice mixes. In some stores, you can also buy ready-made organic vegetable broth in cartons; I love that. When you buy organic stock in powder or cubes you need to check the guidelines as to how much you should use. Usually it is around 1 tbsp or one cube for 500ml of water so I follow those measurements in my recipes.

> Remember, in all my recipes, I favour organic produce, use ripe fruits, and wash and dry fresh fruits and vegetables before I start.

Simple broccoli soup

A very easy delicious broccoli soup that you can turn into a cauliflower soup! I buy coconut milk in cartons with no preservatives or thickeners.

Serves 2–3
1 leek
1 bay leaf
1 tbsp butter
3 tbsp water
About 500g broccoli or cauliflower
1 tsp sea salt
300ml water
300ml coconut milk
1 cube or 1 tbsp organic yeast- and MSG-free vegetable stock
Sea salt (optional)
A little extra butter or coconut cream (optional)

◆ Chop the leek, then put it in a medium-sized pan with the bay leaf, butter and water and heat gently until fragrant.
◆ Chop the broccoli and add it to the saucepan with the rest of the ingredients. Let it boil over low heat for about 10–15 minutes, keeping the lid on.
◆ Then purée with a hand-held blender in the pan. Use sea salt and even a little butter or coconut cream to taste.

Lovely Suleila's butternut soup

This is one of my favourites!

Serves 4

1 onion or 2 leeks
2 garlic cloves
1–2 tbsp organic butter
1 tbsp cumin powder
2 bay leaves
About 5 tbsp water
1 butternut squash
1 litre organic yeast- and MSG-free chicken or vegetable broth
3 tbsp organic tomato paste
Sea salt and black pepper to taste
60ml cream or coconut cream or milk

- Peel and chop the onion or leeks and garlic.
- In a rather large pot or saucepan over a medium heat, gently cook the onions or leeks and the garlic along with the spices, cumin and bay leaf in the butter until fragrant. I also always add a little water to keep the butter from heating too much.
- Meanwhile, peel the butternut squash and chop it into cubes.
- Turn down the heat. Add the squash to the saucepan as well as the stock and tomato paste. Bring to a boil and cook until the butternut squash cubes are tender, or around 15–20 minutes.
- Turn off the heat, discard the bay leaf and purée the soup until smooth. Season with salt and pepper, add the cream and gently reheat if necessary. Enjoy!

- On a good day, it is nice to serve some croûtons with this butternut soup, but not necessary.
- It is very easy to skip the cream every now and then in recipes and use coconut milk (I get it in cartons, not tin cans); it tastes amazing and feels much lighter in your stomach!

Mexican chicken soup with nachos, soured cream and shredded cheese

This is perfect for a Saturday evening supper. You can include sweet potato if you like – I love sweet potato!

Serves 4–5

400g organic chicken breasts (you can skip the chicken and use 2 sweet potatoes instead)
1 red pepper
½ red or green chilli, deseeded (optional)
1 yellow onion
2 tsp paprika (I love sweet paprika)
100ml water
1 sweet potato (if I skip the chicken I use around 2 sweet potatoes, depending on size)
6 tomatoes
3 tbsp organic tomato paste
1 litre water
1 tsp sea salt
2 cubes or 2 tbsp organic yeast- and MSG-free vegetable stock
200ml organic mild salsa or taco sauce
200ml coconut milk or 100g organic cream cheese
Organic plain nachos, soured cream and shredded organic full-fat cheese, to serve

♦ Cut the chicken into bite-size pieces and remember to never let raw chicken (or any meat) come in contact with raw vegetables, fruits or salad. It's best to have a separate cutting board which is used only for raw meat.
♦ Deseed and chop the pepper and chilli and peel and chop the onion into bite-size pieces.
♦ In a rather large saucepan, gently simmer the chicken, pepper, chilli and onion along with the paprika in the 100ml water while you prepare the rest of the recipe.
♦ Peel the sweet potatoes and tomatoes, chop them and add them to the saucepan. Add the tomato paste, water, sea salt and stock and simmer over a low heat for about 20 minutes.
♦ Finally you add the salsa and coconut milk or cream cheese and

heat through, then you serve it with organic plain nachos, soured cream and any shredded organic full fat cheese you like (I often use mozzarella).

- I buy my coconut milk in cartons with no preservatives or thickeners.

Lentil and vegetable soup

Serves 4
1 yellow onion
50–100ml water
1 tbsp paprika
1 bay leaf
3 garlic cloves
1 red pepper
1 sweet potato
1 courgette
400g fresh tomatoes or passata
200g red lentils
400ml coconut milk
500ml water
3 cubes or 3 tbsp organic yeast- and MSG-free vegetable stock

- Peel and chop the onion and put it in a pan with the water, paprika, bay leaf and garlic. Heat gently until fragrant, while you prepare the rest of the ingredients.
- Deseed and chop the red pepper, peel and chop the sweet potato, chop the courgette and tomatoes, and wash the lentils. Add them to the pan with the coconut milk and water, bring to the boil, then simmer over a low heat for around 20 minutes, keeping the lid on.
- After 20 minutes you can either blend it with your hand-held blender or leave it as it is!

- If you can buy kombu, which is kelp or seaweed, it is nice to put a 10cm strip into the pot. It makes the digestion of the lentils easier for your body.

Italian vegetable soup

This is awesome with some freshly grated Parmesan!

Serves 4

1 yellow onion
2 garlic cloves
50–100ml water
2 tsp marjoram
½ celeriac (it looks ugly but tastes wonderful in this soup!)
3 carrots, sweet potato or butternut squash
½ cauliflower
1 litre water
400g fresh tomatoes or passata
3 tbsp organic tomato paste
3–4 cubes or 3–4 tbsp organic yeast- and MSG-free vegetable stock
200g wholewheat spelt pasta or gluten-free pasta
Freshly grated Parmesan cheese (optional)
Chopped fresh parsley or basil (optional)

- Chop the onion and garlic and put them into a pan with the 100ml water and marjoram. Heat gently while you prepare the rest of the ingredients.
- Peel the celeriac and the carrots, potato or squash, if necessary, and cut into bite-size pieces. Chop the cauliflower into similar-sized pieces. Put everything one by one in the pan except the pasta, Parmesan and herbs and let boil over a low heat for around 10 minutes.
- Then add the pasta and cook for a further 10 minutes. I love it to serve it with some Parmesan and fresh herbs sprinkled over the top.

- Simply change the vegetables according to seasons.
- If you keep the spices then the soup won't change all that much, it's just nice to have variety.

Hummus with sundried tomatoes
Homemade hummus ... hhhhhhmmmmm!

Serves 4

400g cooked chickpeas
A few sundried tomatoes (optional)
Parsley
Orange juice from 1 orange (optional)
Juice of ½ lemon or lime
2 tbsp organic tahini
1–2 tbsp organic tamari sauce
1 tsp cumin, and 1 tsp paprika
1–2 garlic cloves
Sea salt and freshly ground black pepper
Cold-pressed olive oil to thin it to the desired consistency

◆ Put all ingredients in a food processor or blender and blend well.

● This keeps in the fridge for about 3-4 days.

> Tamari sauce is made with more soybeans than ordinary soy sauce, resulting in a smoother and more balanced flavour. Your typical soy sauce, shoyu, has wheat in it, which is done, I think, to increase production. With mass production, the manufacturers somewhere along the line realised that fermenting soya beans with wheat was a far cheaper process than making the sauce from pure soya. But always read the label, it should only say soya beans, water, sea salt. I also always go for an organic brand.

Porridges
When your children no longer want to eat baby porridge (finely ground and cooked grains) and want to start chewing their food, there is no need to discard good healthy varieties of grains and porridges. You simply start boiling the whole varieties. It is healthy, cheap, quick and easy. By soaking your grains overnight you cut down on boiling time by around half. What also happens when you soak whole grains is that they become more alkalizing for your body and more easily digested.

Oat porridge

Serves 2
100g organic rolled oats
250–300ml water and/or organic rice milk

◆ Simply boil the oats and water/rice milk together for about 2–3 minutes, using a low heat. Add water or milk if necessary to thin or cool it down.
◆ And then you can enjoy it with whatever you like.

● My daughter likes rice milk or organic milk, cinnamon, apple bits and palm sugar. My son sometimes adds raisins as well (you can also cook a few raisins with the porridge). You will soon find your own version!
● This keeps in the fridge for around 3 days.
Soaked chia seeds are also nice in the oat porridge.

> If you are using whole grain oats (uncut) you have to boil them for 40 minutes just like the brown rice. And you can let them stand overnight after boiling them for about 20 minutes in the evening. And you will have a wonderful porridge waiting for you in the morning that you only need to boil for a short time (maybe 10 minutes or so). You can also cook them with apple bits, pears, dates, apricots, ground cinnamon or vanilla. In short, anything you fancy!

Rice porridge

Serves 2–3
100g organic brown rice
250ml water
2 dates (optional)
100–200ml organic rice milk or other milk you prefer
Pinch of vanilla powder (optional)
Pinch of sea salt (optional)
Pinch of ground cinnamon

◆ Rinse the brown rice and put in a pan with the water and dates, if you like a sweet flavour. Let it boil and then lower the heat and let it simmer for about 40 minutes, adding extra boiling water if needed.
◆ Add the milk, with the vanilla and salt, if using, and let simmer slowly for about 10–20 minutes longer.
◆ Then you serve this sprinkled with the cinnamon.

• The dates give it a sweet taste but in case you or your children want it sweeter, you can use a little bit of organic palm or cane sugar.
• You can also put some dried fruit on it or apple bits, whatever you love!
• I sometimes cook the rice in water before I go to bed for about 15–20 minutes. It is very clever to have a clock in the kitchen that bleeps at you when time is up so you don't forget the rice porridge on the hot stove. Then when the time is up, I turn off the heat and let the pot stand overnight with the lid on. The day after, the rice is almost cooked (from being in the heat) and you only have to heat it up with some milk and serve with cinnamon and whatever else you like.
• Cooked rice keeps in the fridge for about 3 days. It can come in handy to have cooked rice in the fridge to be able to make a quick breakfast, lunch or dinner.
• Leftover rice porridge can also be mixed with whipped cream, quality vanilla and some nice organic syrup or jam for a delicious dessert that tastes like Christmas pudding!

I love quinoa!

Look at the video of how to make this porridge at www.pureebba.com.

Serves 2–3
100g whole quinoa
250ml water
A little lemon olive oil
Chopped mango or apple, or fresh herbs, to serve

◆ I rinse my quinoa with boiled water or soak it for a few hours.
◆ I then rinse it in a sieve and boil for 10–15 minutes using a low heat. Use only around 200ml water if the quinoa has been soaked.
◆ I eat my quinoa with lemon olive oil and apple or mango bits. It is so lovely! My Hanna also loves it like that.

• Quinoa is also good mixed in soups and stews and some simply eat it as a side dish and then you can mix it with olive oil, garlic, red onions, sundried tomatoes, olives, mango bits, fresh herb, and so on. You can also add it to your salad.
• Quinoa is naturally gluten-free.
• It is truly delicious to cook ½ cup quinoa in water with ½–1 tbsp organic yeast- and MSG-free vegetable stock. When the quinoa is cooked, I add some lemon juice, chopped cucumber and carrot, fresh herbs if I have them, diced red onion, tomatoes (sundried are also nice), ripe mango bits even feta cheese, but it's all up to you. I dress it with some olive oil, sea salt and pepper. It's wonderful as a side dish and also as a meal in itself.

Very easy wholewheat spelt pasta

When you have very little time or energy to make dinner, it is just fine to simply boil organic wholewheat pasta or gluten-free pasta and serve with garlic olive oil and sea salt, for instance.

Serves 2–4
1 litre water
200g wholewheat spelt pasta
½ tbsp cold-pressed olive oil or coconut oil

◆ Heat the water in a medium-sized saucepan. When it starts boiling, add the pasta and the oil and stir. Let the pasta boil over a low heat with the lid half on for about 10 minutes (check the label on the pasta you are using for guidelines as to how many minutes it needs to be cooked).
◆ Drain the pasta in a colander and then you can serve it with anything you like:
- Organic tomato sauce
- Red pesto
- Green pesto
- Raw vegetables, like cucumber, courgette and/or carrot strips
- Organic salad (I highly recommend organic salad)
- Olives
- Parmesan
- Goat cheese
- Anything goes and this takes very little time.

Very easy homemade red pesto

Makes about 300ml
1 jar sundried tomatoes (I recommend organic or without
  preservatives)
2 garlic cloves
75g macadamia nuts or pine nuts
100–150ml cold-pressed olive oil
1 handful of fresh basil (optional)
70g freshly grated Parmesan cheese
1 tbsp lemon or lime juice
Sea salt and black pepper to taste

◆ Usually I discard the oil from the sundried tomatoes, but if it is
   organic and has no preservatives, I use it in the pesto or my
   salad dressing.
◆ Simply blend all the ingredients together and enjoy on bread, on
   your pasta, pizza, whatever.

• This should keep in the fridge for about 4 days in a clean glass
   jar with a lid.
• This is delicious on bread with mozzarella cheese and fresh
   tomatoes.
• You can add 1 tbsp of goji berries to this pesto as well!

Very easy homemade green pesto

If you don't have quite enough basil, you can always make up for it with a little rocket or other green salad, which is best if it is organic or homegrown.

Makes about 300ml
Around 50g fresh basil
50g macadamia nuts or pine nuts
2 garlic cloves
70g freshly grated Parmesan cheese
100–150ml cold-pressed olive oil
1 tbsp lemon or lime juice
Sea salt and black pepper, to taste

◆ Simply purée all the ingredients in a food processor or using your measuring jug and hand-held blender.

● This should keep in the fridge for about 3 days in a clean glass jar with a lid.
● You can also skip the Parmesan and make a raw green pesto. Simply add 2 stoned dates or equal amounts of cranberries (around 2 tbsp) instead of the Parmesan.
● You can use any nuts you like: walnuts, pine, cashew, macadamia, Brazil nuts, or whatever.
● This tastes wonderful with wholewheat pasta or spaghetti as a quick dinner. This is also truly amazing with vegetarian lasagne, Mexican medley, chicken salad and as a spread for bread or crackers (I love the gluten-free ones) along with, for instance, ripe tomatoes and mozzarella. Enjoy!
● I also love a handful (or more) of organic sundried tomatoes in my green pesto!

Mexican vegetable medley

Serves 4

1 large or 2 small onions (I often use one red and one yellow)
3 garlic cloves
2 red or orange peppers
½ fresh chilli, deseeded (optional)
50–100ml water
1½ tsp ground cumin
½–1 tsp ground cinnamon
4 carrots or an equal amount of butternut squash
1 sweet potato
1–2 tbsp lemon juice
400ml coconut milk
8 tbsp organic tomato paste
1 tsp sea salt
1 glass jar cooked organic kidney beans (around 300–400g) rinsed in a
   colander with fresh water (optional)
1–2 handfuls of fresh basil (optional)
Taco shells, avocado lime salsa and soured cream, to serve

◆ Peel and chop the onions and garlic. Deseed and chop the
   pepper and chilli.
◆ Sauté in the water with the spices while you prepare the rest of
   the ingredients.
◆ Peel the carrots, if necessary, and chop them. Peel and chop the
   sweet potato, and cut it into bite-size pieces.
◆ Add them to the pan and simmer over low heat for about 15
   minutes, keeping the lid on.
◆ When ready, add some chopped fresh basil and serve in organic
   taco shells with avocado lime salsa and soured cream.

• To make an avocado lime salsa, simply peel, stone and mash an
   avocado with some lime juice, chopped red onions and sea salt.
• If you are using kidney beans, rinse them in a colander under
   cold water and add them to the pan with the rest of the
   ingredients to warm through.
• You can easily purée a little bit of this lovely dish for your baby
   (over 1 year) with some avocado and soured cream.

Vegetarian bolognese

This is such a tasty recipe, you will be amazed. One little friend of mine had this when visiting us and asked her mum if she could have this for dinner on Christmas Eve! Serve this with some wholewheat spelt spaghetti and a salad.

Serves 6
1 big or 2 small yellow onions
3 garlic cloves
50–100ml water
2 bay leaves
2 tsp oregano
2 tsp basil
1 tsp sea salt
1 sweet potato
130g brown lentils, the ones you only need to cook for 30 minutes (they
  are very small)
400–500g fresh tomatoes or passata
400ml coconut milk (I get it in cartons with no preservatives or
  thickeners, etc.)
100ml water
3 tbsp organic tomato paste
1 cube or 1 tbsp organic yeast- and MSG-free stock

- Peel and chop the onion and garlic.
- Sauté in the water in a large pan with the bay leaves, oregano, basil and sea salt while you prepare the rest.
- Peel and chop the sweet potato. Rinse the lentils in a colander. If you use fresh whole tomatoes I recommend ripe ones (very red!), dice them.
- Put the rest of the ingredients into the pan and let it boil on low heat for about 30 minutes with the lid on.

- For small children it is easy to purée this and use as a thick sauce with spaghetti.

Vegetable lasagne

This is very easy to make, so do not let the long list of ingredients scare you away! Serve it with green pesto and a nice salad and you will loooove me afterwards!

Serves 6

1–2 onions
4 garlic cloves
½ red chili, deseeded
1 red pepper
50–100ml water
3 tsp oregano
3 tsp marjoram
2 tsp paprika
2 bay leaves
Sea salt, to taste
1 sweet potato or 1 butternut squash or a little bit of both, washed,
   peeled and cut into bite-size pieces
2 courgettes
2 carrots
500g ripe (very red) tomatoes or passata
3–4 tbsp organic tomato purée
For the sauce
300g mozzarella or any organic full-fat cheese you like
500–600ml coconut milk
350g wholewheat lasagne sheets

- Peel and chop the onions and garlic. Deseed and chop the chilli and pepper.
- Using a fairly big pan, heat them in the water with the herbs and salt for a few minutes over a low heat while you prepare the rest of the ingredients.
- Peel and chop with sweet potato or squash. Cut the courgettes into bite-size pieces. Peel the carrots, if necessary, and cut into bite-size pieces. Chop the tomatoes.
- Add to the pan and let this boil over a low heat for about 20–30 minutes, keeping the lid on.
- Heat your oven to 200°C/400°F/Gas 6.

◆ To make the sauce, shred the mozzarella and mix with the coconut milk.
◆ In a fairly big oven dish, layer the casserole first, then the lasagne sheets (I use from whole spelt) and then the white sauce (coconut milk and mozzarella mixture) and repeat until nothing is left. Bake in the oven for around 25 minutes.

● It is a must to serve basil pesto with this lasagne! (page 142)

My favourite chicken salad

I love this salad wholeheartedly. If you love Parmesan cheese, you simply have to try it! I always buy organic bread, such as Italian Ciabatta, with no additives or preservatives if possible.

Serves 4
200g organic green salad leaves
3–4 garlic cloves
8 tbsp olive oil
4 tbsp lemon juice
Sea salt
Black pepper (optional)
150g freshly grated Parmesan cheese (oh yes!)
3–4 organic chicken breasts
A little coconut oil
For the bread
4 garlic cloves (if you looove garlic, use some more!)
100g soft organic butter, at room temperature
5–6 tbsp cold-pressed olive oil
Chopped fresh parsley (optional)
Freshly grated Parmesan cheese
1 ciabatta bread or baguette loaf, sliced almost through to the base

- Put the salad in a bowl.
- Crush the garlic and mix with the olive oil, lemon juice, sea salt and black pepper, if using, in a glass or jar. Pour over the salad and sprinkle with the Parmesan.
- Now cut the chicken into bite-size pieces and sauté using with the coconut oil over a low heat. You could also grill the chicken or bake the chicken breasts in the oven for 25–35 minutes at 180°C /360°F/Gas 4. When the chicken is cooked, cut it in bite-size bits and throw over the salad.
- To make the bread, peel the garlic. Purée the butter with the garlic, olive oil and parsley. Spread a thick layer on to the bread slices and put it into the oven at 150°C/300°F/Gas 2 for just a few minutes or until you see the bread has started taking in all the butter and olive oil. I use my oven tray under the bread slices and baking paper. Take out the bread and grate the Parmesan cheese over it. Serve immediately with the chicken salad.

- You can also just heat the sliced bread in the oven and then spread the flavoured butter on the warm bread and serve with the Parmesan on top!

Homemade garlic oil

Simply press 4–5 garlic cloves into a glass jar and pour cold-pressed organic olive oil into the jar (around 100ml). Put the lid on and keep it in the fridge. I use only the oil for my kids and not the garlic that sits at the bottom of the jar! Then you simply add more olive oil when it is finished and after a month or so I make a new one (I press new garlic into a new jar and start all over again). I always keep my garlic oil in the fridge. It is lovely poured over pizzas, pasta, vegetable soups, breads etc. and a great way to get healthy essential fats into your diet. We all need the right kind of fat in order to be happy and healthy! Remember, the trick is to use cold-pressed oils raw, and to pour them over your food after you have cooked it.

Cold-pressed vegetable oils are very sensitive to heat, light and air and in the case of extreme heat (as in frying) they can become toxic. It is best to fry with just water when possible and when not, you can use cold-pressed coconut oil, butter or ghee, and occasionally olive oil.

> I truly believe that our future must be organic; otherwise there will be no future for us on this planet.

Cod or halibut tasty fish balls

With this, I serve melted butter and steamed or fresh vegetables and/or potatoes.

Serves 4–6

1 yellow onion
700–800g cod, halibut or other white fish
1 large or 2 small organic or free-range eggs (optional) or 4 tbsp water
1/2 cube or 1/2 tbsp organic yeast- and MSG-free stock
4 tbsp hot water
About 100–200g wholewheat spelt (or other organic wheat you like)
Coconut oil or ghee, for frying

♦ Peel and chop the onion. Mash the fish with the onion in a food processor. Put the mixture into a bowl and add the eggs, if using, or water. Stir with a spatula.

♦ Dissolve the stock in the hot water and add it to the bowl. Stir again.

♦ Divide this into 4 pieces and take one piece out. Fill the gap up with wholewheat spelt. Put the part you took out back in the bowl and mix everything together until you have a stiff dough, You can add water if you need it. If you have time, keep this in the fridge for about 30 minutes. Make round balls (not too big/high), with an ice-cream scoop.

♦ Fry them in a little coconut oil over low heat (slow cooking!) for a few minutes or until golden on all sides. Then you have two options. One is to pour water into the pan so that it covers the lower half of the fish balls, put the lid on and turn off the heat. Then you simply let them cook there slowly for further 5–10 minutes or until cooked all through. The other option is to put them in an oven tray, on baking paper into a 160°C/320°F/Gas 3 oven and bake them for around 5–10 minutes or until cooked all through.

● You can easily freeze this mixture for 2 months. And when you want to use it, let it defrost in the fridge overnight.

● These fish balls are extremely delicious and easy to make. You can also put some finely shredded vegetables like carrots or kale into the fish mixture.

● You can also use bean purée instead of some of the fish.

In my experience, children love simple things. I recommend trying for example steamed white fish (from 9 months but later if allergy runs in the family) with some organic cooked potatoes or sweet potatoes or other steamed vegetables. It is really good mashed with some organic butter. You will love it too. This is a very traditional dinner among families in Iceland.

Friday pizza

This is the best pizza ever, and yet so healthy. First I'd like to tell you that it takes very little time to make a pizza like this one because it contains cream of tartar instead of yeast. That is why you won't be bloated after eating it either. Yeast is not really the best thing for healthy intestinal flora. I use spelt flour in my pizza. Spelt is much gentler on the stomach than wheat and more easily digested since it is water-soluble. It also contains more protein than wheat. I make my pizza base very thin! It will take you no more than 20 minutes to make 2–3 (depending how well you stretch them) large pizzas! Good luck on pizza night and have fun!

Makes 2–3 large pizzas
*250g spelt (for beginners I would use fine and whole fifty/fifty, I usually
only use wholewheat spelt for my pizza)*
3 tsp cream of tartar
1 tsp sea salt
2 tsp oregano (optional)
3 tbsp cold-pressed olive oil or coconut oil
About 130–150ml hot water

For the topping
8 tbsp organic ketchup
8 tbsp organic tomato purée
1 tsp chopped fresh oregano or marjoram (optional)
100g mozzarella cheese
Garlic olive oil (optional)

◆ Blend the dry ingredients together and mix in the hot water. Make dough using a spoon first and then your hands. (All this takes around 3 minutes.)
◆ Then I use a little fine spelt to roll out thin pizzas with a rolling pin. This makes for 2–3 large pizzas at the size of an oven plate, depending on how thin/thick you make them. Place on baking sheets lined with baking parchment and bake them for about 5 minutes.
◆ When they come out of the oven you simply put on it whatever you want. My favourite topping is made by mixing equal quantities of ketchup and tomato purée in a bowl. I put this on

Too expensive?
Keep in mind
that you eat less
and waste less
when you buy
and eat good
quality food.

the pizzas – a lot of it! Then for my kids I simply just put grated mozzarella and throw the pizza in the oven again for about 4–5 minutes. When they come out I pour garlic olive oil over them and serve!

- For me and my husband, I often put diced ripe tomatoes on top (very red, they ripen at room temperature) and maybe some other vegetables I like. It is very nice to bake courgette slices, pumpkin or some other vegetables you like for around 20 minutes and put them on your pizza. Then I add the grated mozzarella. And when they come out of the oven I sprinkle with lots of homemade garlic oil and fresh basil and fresh rocket.
- I also like sundried tomatoes and Parmesan. You will soon find your own version!
- I usually get my children to eat a little salad with it too.
- Small hands can definitely help out and if you don't like the idea of spelt all over your floor you can negotiate that they can spread the sauce and the cheese instead.
- You can substitute some of the spelt flour (50g) with rice flour or buckwheat flour (gluten-free) and you can also add some sesame seeds or finely ground sunflower seeds to the dough … all up to you!

Lovely salad dressing

This will make you want to eat loads of green salad!

Makes about 150ml

100ml organic cold-pressed olive oil
2 tbsp balsamic vinegar or 4 tbsp organic apple cider vinegar (you can
  also use lemon or lime juice)
1 tbsp organic honey, maple syrup, raw agave nectar or yacon syrup
  (more if you want)
1 tbsp organic mustard (or more but optional)
Pinch of sea salt (pepper if you like)
1 tsp acai powder (optional)

◆ Mix all the ingredients together in your blender. Pour over your
  salad and enjoy.

● Walnuts in the salad go well with this dressing.
● Optionally, you can add fresh basil – it's wonderful!

> Many think that a salad is something you only enjoy with your lunch or dinner but you can have salad for breakfast for that matter. Organic salad is loaded with wonderfully nutritious ingredients for anybody. I often put a little in my children's shakes and purées because I am so devious. I also want to tell you to try and put chopped dates in your salad or sulphur-free cranberries, fresh walnuts or other seeds and nuts, such as mango, papaya, pineapple and all the other stuff you can think of. When I have guests I often put Parmesan as well or fresh mozzarella and tomatoes in a salad. You can also go crazy when nice berries are in season and put them in too! Your body will thank you immensely if you start eating green salad with or before your cooked food. It will help your digestion since it is raw and contains all the enzymes that are destroyed through cooking.
>
> Plus it will help your body (the vitamin C) to absorb iron from your food better. All the raw green food from the plant kingdom contains a lot of protein, vitamin C, iron and calcium, for instance. And to grow your own salad is of course very easy, not to mention clever … saves money and a trip to the grocery store!

Mango chutney chicken
This is another favourite!

Serves 4
4–5 organic chicken breasts
7 garlic cloves
50ml water
1 tbsp curry powder, (more if you like)
Sea salt and freshly ground black pepper
½ jar quality mango chutney (around 150g)
250ml organic cream or coconut milk

◆ Cut the chicken breasts into bite-size pieces (remember to use a special cutting board for raw meat and even better a special one just for raw chicken).
◆ Peel and chop the garlic and 'fry' it in a little water using a low heat with the chicken and curry powder until the chicken is cooked through. Add the mango chutney and cream or coconut milk. Let this boil, using a low heat, for around 30-40 minutes.

• Season again with sea salt, pepper and mango chutney to taste. Using scissors I chop some fresh coriander over this dish when ready, then I serve it with organic brown rice and a salad.

Fajitas

Another favourite dish at my house, this is a recipe from Raw Solla. She can do it all – raw, vegan, vegetarian – as long as it is healthy, wholesome food! This is also easy to prepare and ever so delicious. Baking your own tortilla bread makes all the difference not only nutritionally but also taste wise. Wholewheat spelt (and wholewheat) has got so much more flavour than white wheat. You wouldn't believe it so don't be afraid and give it a try!

Serves 4

*250g wholewheat spelt (beginners can use 50/50 wholewheat spelt and
   fine spelt)*
2–4 tbsp sesame seeds (optional but oh, so lovely)
1 tsp sea salt
50ml cold-pressed olive oil or coconut oil
150–175 ml hot water

◆ Mix the dry ingredients and then add the oil and the water. I use a spoon first (because the water is so hot) and then I simply use my nature's forks (my hands!) and make a dough roll (add more water if you need more). Then I cut it into around 8–10 pieces and flatten them quite thin using white spelt to prevent sticking and a rolling pin so they will look something like store bought tortilla breads!
◆ Then I simply bake them on a dry pan (not Teflon!) with no oil or water (dry) for about 1 minute each side. Watch the heat!
◆ When this is ready I simply put them on a dish and on our dinner table and serve with it some of this:
● Organic red or green pesto
● Cucumber, cut into strips
● Carrots, cut into strips
● Salad
● Basil leaves
● Mozzarella, cut into strips
● Sundried tomatoes
● Avocado, peeled, stoned and cut into strips and usually I squeeze lime juice over it or I make guacamole
● Cherry tomatoes, cut into half and seasoned with cut garlic, olive oil and sea salt

- Organic grilled chicken
- Organic salsa sauce
- Soured cream
- And anything else you may think of, so everybody can use what they like in their tortilla pancake!

You can also bake them on a baking sheet in the oven at around 180°C/350°F/Gas 4.

Stroganoff

This is such a lovely dish from my mother's sister, Gudrun. She makes wonderful food and this is one of our favourite dishes. I do not eat a lot of meat but when I do I buy organic.

Serves 4

2 onions
100g butter
400–500g organic beef, cut into 1 x 4cm strips
2 tbsp tomato purée
1–2 tsp good organic mustard (like Dijon)
200ml water
185g soured cream
Salt and black pepper

◆ Peel and chop the onions.
◆ Melt the butter in a medium-sized saucepan and fry the onions until fragrant using a low heat.
◆ Add the beef and stir for a few minutes.
◆ Then add the tomato purée, mustard and water. Simmer over a low heat until the meat is tender or for around 50 minutes.
◆ Then you add the soured cream and you can use salt and pepper to taste.

• I love this with cucumbers and a green salad.
• Many also love it with brown rice or quinoa.

Mozzarella and tomato salad

Serves 4

About 300g fresh mozzarella
3–4 ripe, very red, tomatoes
A good handful of basil leaves
Olive oil
Sea salt and black pepper
Balsamic vinegar

◆ Simply dice the mozzarella and the tomatoes and arrange them alternately on a dish. Decorate with basil leaves and pour over olive oil, balsamic vinegar and a little sea salt and black pepper. Optionally you can add some quality olives … Enjoy!

Eggs can make such a nice, nutritious and yet quick meal. I always opt for organic ones.

Fried eggs

When your babies have reached 12 months, you can occasionally serve them eggs. You simply use coconut oil and a pan or a small pot. For 2 eggs you only need about 1 tsp coconut oil. Use low heat. Simply heat the egg (I stir it while it is cooking) until done (I like mine medium done). Then I use Himalaya salt to season it. Then you cut it for your baby to enjoy with their fingers or a spoon.

Egg salad

It is also very nice to make an egg salad by mixing together mayonnaise from a health store and a hard-boiled egg and cucumber.

How to hard-boil an egg

You boil water in a pot, enough to cover the egg once it is in it. When the water boils you turn down the heat a bit and put your egg in – I use a spoon to do that. And then you boil your egg for about 9–10 minutes. When the time is up, you turn off the heat and pour cold water into the pot over the egg. This will prevent the egg from cooking further and it lets it cool down a bit. Now you only have to remove the eggshell and enjoy your egg!

You can keep cooked eggs in your fridge for around 2–3 days.

Sweet Things and Parties

At children's birthday parties it is very easy to make refreshments that are truly delicious and yet healthy! Honestly! Here I give you my best ones that I use so much myself and love dearly!

If you have old recipes you really cherish you can always change them for the better. Use organic unbleached wheat or organic spelt flour instead of the white refined (often bleached) wheat flour. You can use organic unrefined cane sugar, palm sugar, organic agave nectar, honey or maple syrup instead of the white sugar. And actually you can usually cut the sugar amount by one third (even half!) without anybody noticing it!

Guidelines to making recipes healthier

Instead of margarine, which has trans fats in it (very unhealthy), you can use organic butter. You can also use coconut oil instead of margarine or butter and you can use less (see chart on next page). And furthermore, homemade treats are always so much healthier than store bought candy, which is loaded with sugar and all kinds of artificial flavourings, additives, and the list goes on. Children go to parties to play and have fun – not to eat! That is more the grown-up style. I also recommend you offer water at parties and diluted pure fruit juice instead of fizzy drinks. And fruits, waffles, pancakes, homemade pizza, homemade ice-cream and home baked breads look great and taste amazing at any party!

When you are baking it is very easy to tweak recipes here and there, just a little, to make them healthier for you and your loved ones. When you use quality ingredients they will only get better, I promise you. I do this all the time. Here are some guidelines to help you out.

Remember that most of us can easily tolerate eating unhealthy foods once in a while. It is the day-to-day meals that count, not the exceptions. Also bear in mind that we can only control how we shop and what we cook in our own household. My point is, be kind to people like grandma and grandpa. I believe they should be allowed to spoil their grandchildren (when they have discovered treats that is, often not until 2–3 years old!) sometimes with ice-cream or cakes. They need leverage! :-) My mother makes healthy waffles for her grandchildren, she also gives them high-quality dark chocolate from time to time, she buys ice-cream with no additives and sometimes she bakes them a cake using quality ingredients. But most of all she and my dad love them more than anything and give them their undivided attention while they are visiting. I am sure they add to their IQ and mental health!

For cakes, for 100g wheat flour, substitute:
100g organic fine spelt flour
75g organic fine spelt flour and 25g ground almonds, desiccated coconut, rice flour or buckwheat flour, for example
50g organic whole spelt/wheat flour and 50g organic fine spelt/wheat flour
For breads, for 100g wheat flour, substitute:
100g whole spelt flour
75g whole spelt flour and 25g ground almonds, ground nuts or seeds or leftover almond (nut/seed) pulp, desiccated coconut, rice flour or buckwheat, for example
For 100g refined sugar, substitute:
50–75g raw organic cane sugar
125g date purée
50g organic raw honey
50g organic agave nectar
50g organic maple syrup
50–75g organic palm sugar
Also try using very ripe bananas in cake recipes. 100g sugar would be 3–4 very ripe bananas.
For 100g margarine, substitute:
100g organic pure butter
50g organic pure butter and 50g organic cream
50–75g organic cold-pressed coconut oil
40g organic pure butter and 40g organic cold-pressed coconut oil

Apple tart
This is quick and easy to prepare and tastes amazing!

Serves 4
3–4 apples

For the dough
3 organic eggs
75g organic palm sugar or agave nectar
75g organic cold-pressed coconut oil
130g spelt flour (whole or fine or fifty/fifty)
1 tbsp ground cinnamon
1–2 tbsp lemon or lime juice
2 tsp cream of tartar
Fresh cream and seasonal berries, to serve

◆ Heat your oven to 180°C/350°F/Gas 4.
◆ Peel, core and chop the apples into rather small pieces. Put them in a 26–28cm ceramic cake mould and keep them in the oven while you prepare the dough.
◆ First mix the eggs with the palm sugar or agave until quite fluffy and light. Add the remaining ingredients and mix well but gently.
◆ Take the apples out of the oven. Pour the dough mixture over the apples and bake in the oven for around 20 minutes.
◆ Enjoy with whipped cream and maybe some fresh seasonal fruits and berries.

Healthy chocolate squares

I often use as a prize for those who eat their dinner without complaining. Keep your coconut oil at room temperature so it is soft when you need to use it.

Makes approximately 15 pieces
150g fresh dates, stoned
5 tbsp organic (raw) cacao
5 tbsp organic cold-pressed coconut oil
100g desiccated coconut

◆ Using your processor, blend the dates, cacao, coconut oil and half of the desiccated coconut together until quite well puréed.
◆ With your hands, make squares or balls from the mixture and dip them in the remaining desiccated coconut.

● These keep in the fridge for a long time for anybody and everybody to enjoy at any time.
● You may like to add 2–3 tbsp soaked chia seeds into the recipe.

Egg-free chocolate cake

This is our favourite birthday cake ever and quick and easy to do as well. You can ice it with Easy chocolate spread on page 171.

Makes two 24cm cakes
200g organic palm or cane sugar
500g organic pure yoghurt
300g organic spelt flour (fine and whole fifty/fifty)
6 tbsp organic cocoa powder
3 tsp natron or cream of tartar
150g melted organic butter

◆ Heat the oven to 180°C/360°F/Gas 4.
◆ Mix the sugar and the yoghurt together well.
◆ Add all the other ingredients and mix together. Spoon into two greased and lined 24cm cake tins.
◆ Bake in the oven for 18–20 minutes until well risen and springy.

Gluten-free chocolate cake

Makes a 26cm cake
240g gluten-free flour (I use rice and buckwheat)
3 tsp natron or cream of tartar
1 tsp sea salt
5 tbsp organic cocoa powder
3 organic eggs
120g organic palm or cane sugar
½ tsp vanilla powder (optional)
80g organic butter (or coconut oil)
200ml coconut milk (I get it in cartons with no preservatives or
thickeners, etc. You.can also use organic yoghurt or milk.

- Blend together the flour, cream of tartar, salt and cocoa powder.
- In another bowl, mix the eggs, sugar and vanilla, if using, until light and fluffy.
- Melt the butter and coconut oil together using a low heat.
- Blend together the egg and sugar mixture with the dry ingredients, then add the coconut milk and melted butter and coconut oil and mix slowly. Pour into a greased and lined 26cm cake tin.
- Bake in the oven for 18-20 minutes or until baked through.

- You can then use any chocolate frosting you like for decoration. See the icing on page 171.
- You can always poke cakes and bread with a piece of uncooked spaghetti to see if they are ready. If the spaghetti comes out clean it is baked all the way through.

> I love organic palm sugar. It comes from the coconut palm tree. It is a caramel like crystal sugar and a healthy alternative to white processed sugar found in most cake recipes. It is a naturally low glycemic index food. It has a lower glycemic index than cane sugar, honey and even agave. Organic evaporated palm sugar is especially high in minerals including potassium, magnesium and zinc as well as vitamins B2, B3 and B6. Still, palm sugar should be eaten in moderation, like every other sweet food.

Easy chocolate spread

This can be used on any cake.

Makes enough for 2 cakes

150g icing sugar

100–150ml organic cream, almond milk, coconut milk, rice milk or other type you like (you can also use a little warm water instead of some of the milk)

4 tbsp organic cacao

½ tsp vanilla powder (optional)

◆ Mix the ingredients together and spread on your cake!

● You can reduce the icing sugar by one-third and use lucuma powder or coconut flour instead and use 2–3 drops of chocolate stevia (in liquid form) to sweeten the spread instead (or just organic honey or agave nectar).

Hot cacao

As my children have become older they sometimes ask me nicely to make them hot cacao for breakfast on a Sunday morning, along with spelt bread with lots of organic butter and cheese. We do this especially when we have guests who have slept over.

Serves 2

80ml water

3–4 tbsp organic cacao

3 tbsp organic palm sugar

400–500ml organic milk (any sort you like)

◆ I gently heat the water together with the cacao and palm sugar.
◆ Next I pour in the milk and gently heat (do not boil) until warm enough to drink. If it is a bit too warm, a spoonful of whipped cream will do the trick.

French chocolate cake

It is simply a divine delight – I love it as a dessert when I have guests for dinner because it is sooo delicious but also very quick and easy to prepare.

Makes a 26cm cake
200g organic butter
200g 70 per cent organic chocolate
100g organic agave nectar or organic palm sugar, honey or maple syrup
4 organic eggs
3–4 tbsp fine organic spelt, buckwheat, almond or coconut flour

◆ Heat the oven to 180°C/350°F/Gas 4.
◆ Slowly melt the butter and the chocolate together in a bowl over a pan of boiling water.
◆ Mix the agave and the eggs well together or until fluffy.
◆ Let the chocolate and butter mixture cool a bit if still hot, then carefully mix the two together, stirring as little as possible. Add the flour and bake in a greased and lined 26cm cake tin for about 20–25 minutes. It should be very soft in the middle.

• You can also use leftover pulp from making homemade almond milk instead of the flour.
• You can also add some chopped walnuts or other nuts, even almonds and fresh berries to the mixture before baking.

French chocolate cake frosting

French chocolate cake does not need any spread. I usually sift some icing sugar over it and decorate with fresh berries. But if you like you can use either this or the next icing. It makes the cake more massive and then each bite will weigh heaver in your guests' stomachs – but that means you need less.

Makes enough for one 26cm cake
75g organic butter
150g 70 per cent organic chocolate
1–2 tbsp organic agave nectar or honey

◆ Slowly melt the butter and chocolate together in a bowl over a pan of hot water.
◆ Remove from the heat and then mix in the agave/honey.
◆ Let it cool a bit (not too much though so it won't stiffen up on you again!) and spread on your cake.

Melted cream and chocolate frosting

Makes enough for one 26cm cake
100ml organic cream (or organic milk you like)
100g 70 per cent organic chocolate
A little organic agave nectar or organic raw honey (optional)

◆ Melt the ingredients slowly together in a pan, then allow to cool. Mix in a little organic agave or raw honey if you want it sweeter. Let it cool a bit (not too much to prevent it from stiffening up again) and spread on your cake.

• This spread is also wonderful on waffles.

Cornflake muffins

Really nice and fast cakes for any birthday party!

Makes 10
200g organic dark chocolate
3 tbsp organic butter
3 tbsp organic agave nectar, maple syrup or raw honey
Organic cornflakes, I like buckwheat the most!

◆ Put everything except the cornflakes in a large pan and melt slowly using a low heat. Do not boil!
◆ Add the cornflakes, as many as you like, and stir everything together.
◆ Spoon this mixture into muffin moulds or you could simply put it in one big ceramic cake mould. Freeze and take out 20 minutes or so before serving.

• I also love using 100g organic dark chocolate and 100g organic caramel chocolate.
• You can also decorate a cake with whipped cream on top and fresh berries or fruits.

Helena's date cake

This is one of my all-time favourites, delicious, healthy, quick and easy. It looks amazing and tastes delicious!

Makes a 26cm cake

For the filling
250g fresh dates, stoned
Pure orange juice or pineapple juice (optional)
Water
50g desiccated coconut (optional)
50g chopped nuts (optional)

For the cake
200g wholewheat spelt flour
Pinch of sea salt (optional)
75g cold-pressed coconut oil or 90g organic butter
50ml hot water
Fresh seasonal fruits, nuts or berries, to decorate
Whipped cream or rice-cream, to serve

◆ It is best to start with the filling. Put the dates in a pan with enough juice and water, in roughly equal quantities, to just about cover the dates. Bring to boil using a low heat and then turn off the heat and let it stand with the lid on while you prepare the cake.
◆ Heat your oven to 180°C/360°F/Gas 4.
◆ Put the spelt in a bowl and some sea salt (not necessary if you use butter since it is salty). Add the coconut oil or butter. Rub this together with your fingers. Add the hot water and make a dough-like pastry with your fingers.
◆ Press the dough into a 26cm ceramic cake mould. Prick the dough with a fork here and there and bake in the oven for around 15 minutes. Leave to cool.
◆ When you want to use the filling, purée or mash the dates, mix in the desiccated coconut and chopped nuts or almonds, if you like, and spread on your cake. Decorate with fresh seasonal fruits and berries. I serve whipped cream or rice-cream with it.

• Instead of the wholewheat spelt flour, I often use 150g

buckwheat or almond flour and 50g coconut flour for a gluten-free base and then I only use 70g coconut oil.

And who likes popcorn?

Serves 3
3 tbsp organic cold-pressed coconut oil or high oleic sunflower oil
50g organic popcorn
Sea salt

◆ Put the oil in a large pan and turn up the heat (not quite the highest temperature though!). Add the popcorn, put the lid on and wait until it starts popping, shaking the pan now and again.
◆ Once it calms down a bit (popping less and less), turn off the heat. Once it has almost completely stopped, take it off the hot stove and season it with sea salt. Enjoy!

Gingerbread cookies for Christmas

200g organic wholewheat spelt flour
200g organic fine spelt flour
100g organic cane or palm sugar
2 tsp ground ginger
4 tsp ground cinnamon
2 tsp grated nutmeg
½ tsp black pepper
2–3 tsp natron or bicarbonate of soda
180g soft organic butter
50–100ml organic milk (or other 'milk' and start with 50ml)
2–3 tbsp organic sugar beet syrup or maple syrup

- Mix the dry ingredients together in a large bowl.
- Then add the butter, 50ml of the milk and the syrup, and knead this together well, adding a little more milk if necessary. If you have time, keep it in the fridge for about 30–60 minutes.
- Heat your oven to 200°C/400°F/Gas 6.
- Cut the dough into a few pieces (it's much easier like that) and roll out each one individually to about 5mm thick, using a rolling pin and fine spelt to prevent it sticking.
- Then you can cut out Christmas gingerbread cookies using various cutters like a Christmas tree, star, heart, angels and all the other you find in cutlery shops to make gingerbread cookies for Christmas. Your children will love it.
- Place on lined baking sheets and bake in the oven plate for about 8–10 minutes.

- Keep them in the fridge/freezer in a sealed container.

Cinnamon rolls

Makes about 20–30
200g organic fine spelt flour
150g organic wholewheat spelt flour
4 tsp cream of tartar
1 tsp sea salt
100–150ml warm organic rice milk or milk (and warm water will do
* if you have no milk!)*
3 tbsp organic agave nectar, maple syrup or palm sugar
5 tbsp organic cold-pressed coconut oil or organic butter

For the filling – 3 options
Melted butter and/or coconut oil with ground cinnamon and organic
* palm sugar, maple syrup or agave nectar*
Blueberry jam and ground cinnamon
Apple purée, organic raisins and cinnamon

◆ Heat your oven to 200°C/400°F/Gas 6.
◆ Blend together the flours, cream of tartar and salt.
◆ Heat the milk until warm. Add to the dry ingredients with the
  remaining ingredients and knead to a dough.
◆ Cut the dough in half and roll out each one individually, quite
  thinly, on a floured surface.
◆ Spread with your chosen filling: melted butter and/or coconut
  oil with cinnamon and organic palm sugar, maple syrup or
  agave nectar; blueberry jam and cinnamon; or apple purée,
  organic raisins and cinnamon.
◆ Then you roll this up and cut into around 20–25 pieces.
  Arrange on a lined baking sheet and bake in the oven for about
  10–12 minutes.

My children's favourite muffin recipe

Makes 12–15

3 organic eggs

50g organic palm sugar, raw honey or agave nectar

150g fine spelt flour

2 tsp cream of tartar

100g melted organic butter or around 70g organic cold-pressed coconut oil

½ tsp vanilla powder

75g 70 per cent dark chocolate, grated

◆ Heat your oven to 180°C/350°F/Gas 4.

◆ Mix the sugar and eggs well together until quite fluffy.

◆ Blend in the rest of the ingredients.

◆ Spoon into lined muffin moulds and bake for around 10–15 minutes until springy.

Healthy and delicious chocolate mousse

Always use ripe bananas and do not feed honey to children under 12 months of age.

Serves 4

1 large avocado
1 banana (optional)
3 tbsp organic cold-pressed coconut oil
3 tbsp organic agave nectar or raw honey
3 tbsp organic cacao powder
½ tsp vanilla powder (optional)
Water, organic coconut water or coconut milk to thin it out
Fresh seasonal berries or passion fruit, to serve

- If the coconut oil is too stiff you simply put the jar in hot water (no warmer than 40°C/100°F, though) until it becomes runny or very soft. Then you purée all the ingredients. I usually use my glass measuring jug and hand-held blender.
- Serve it with fresh seasonal berries or passion fruit. If you have time it is nice to put the pudding into the fridge for a while and serve it cold. I can never wait myself though!

- If it is not sweet enough, add a little agave nectar.
- And if it does not have enough cacao flavour, add some more cacao. This recipe can never go wrong!
- For those who don't like banana flavour, just skip it! You might then have to add some more agave since the banana adds to the sweet flavour.

You can see lots of how-to videos, including making waffles, on www.puréebba.com.

Spelt waffles

Waffles are a wonderful way to give your children healthy whole grains. Everybody loves hot bread and that is what a waffle is essentially! And what I love is that it takes only around 6–8 minutes to make waffle dough and then you can start baking, although you do need a waffle iron.

Serves 4

300g organic wholewheat spelt flour
100g organic fine spelt flour
½–1 tsp sea salt
1–2 tsp ground cardamom powder, 1 tsp vanilla powder, 1–2 tsp almond essence or even the juice of 1 lemon
2–3 organic eggs (optional, but without them you'll need to increase the butter or oil to 80g)
600–700ml water and organic rice milk or other milk you prefer
30–40g organic cold-pressed coconut oil, olive oil or organic butter (around 4 tbsp)

- Simply mix the dry ingredients and then work in the remaining ingredients, finishing with the oil or butter, to make a dough like a thick porridge.
- Heat your waffle iron until the light goes out. Add a little of the dough – you'll work out exactly how much after a couple of waffles. Close the waffle iron and the light will come on, then go off when the waffle is cooked.

- I serve my waffles with organic jam, organic agave nectar, maple syrup or melted dark chocolate, fresh seasonal berries and sometimes organic (rice) cream. The possibilities are endless.
- And if you skip the cardamom and the vanilla, you simply have a bread you can enjoy with butter and cheese.
- You could even add some other spices you like, chopped olives, sundried tomatoes … anything you like!

I sometimes throw in my waffle dough, cooked brown rice I have in the fridge or leftover porridge or almond pulp (from making homemade almond milk). Sometimes I add a little bit of coconut flour or desiccated coconut. Waffles always taste great. Anybody can make them and everybody will enjoy them. Optionally you can also skip the eggs and use more oil and some tartar baking powder (around 2 tsp) so it will not stick. You can also put a little coconut oil or butter on the waffle iron before baking each waffle. My mum uses 100g organic butter instead of the coconut or olive oil and no eggs and her waffles are crispier. You can also substitute some or all of the spelt for buckwheat flour (it is naturally gluten-free). I very often use 200g spelt and 200g buckwheat.

Pancakes

Delicious but healthy for you to make any day of the week.

Serves 4
200g organic wholewheat spelt flour
200g organic fine spelt flour or buckwheat flour
2 tsp cream of tartar
Small pinch of sea salt
1–2 tbsp lemon juice
½ tsp vanilla powder or almond essence
2–3 organic eggs
4 tbsp organic cold-pressed coconut oil or organic butter
900ml–1 litre organic rice milk (but you can substitute some of the organic rice milk with water or use other milk you like)

◆ Simply mix the dry ingredients and then add the rest, ending with the oil/butter.
◆ Make the pancakes in a pancake pan over a medium heat, adding a spoonful to the pan and swirling it round to spread the mixture. Cook one side, then flip to the other side.

• Serve them with organic palm or cane sugar and perhaps some cinnamon as well.
• It is also really nice to squeeze a little bit of fresh lemon juice over each pancake after frying.
• I also love jam and cream but then you have to let them cool a bit first.
• You can substitute the fine spelt flour for buckwheat flour, which is gluten-free.

I know from experience that you eat less when eating bread from whole grains than refined (white) ones. This is because the fibre makes you feel full sooner and also because nutritious food in general makes your body and mind feel happy, content and full, while nutrition deficit food leaves us feeling tired and unfulfilled.

The best banana bread

This is a wonderful bread from Raw Solla.

Makes one 900g loaf
200g organic wholewheat spelt flour
3 tsp cream of tartar
1 tsp vanilla powder
150g soft dates, stoned
2 ripe bananas
5 tbsp organic cold-pressed coconut oil
2 organic eggs
50ml organic rice milk or pure yoghurt
Chopped nuts to put on top of the bread before baking

◆ Heat your oven to 180°C /350°F/Gas 4.
◆ Mix the dry ingredients.
◆ Mix the dates and the bananas with the coconut oil in a food processor. Add the eggs and the milk or yoghurt. Mix in with the dry ingredients.
◆ Put in a 900g bread mould, spread the nuts over it and bake for about 45–50 minutes. If you stick uncooked spaghetti into the bread very deeply and it comes out clean, it is ready! Enjoy with some butter.

Snickers raw food cake

You can use any kind of nuts or seeds; I soak mine for a few hours first, but that is not necessary. Keep the coconut oil at room temperature to make it soft. I have yet to meet a person who does not love this cake!

Makes one 26cm cake
100g sesame seeds, cashews or almonds
100g desiccated coconut
150g dates, stoned

For the second layer
200g cashews (I soak mine for a few hours first but it's not necessary)
120ml organic cold-pressed coconut oil
225g organic peanut butter
120ml organic agave nectar or raw honey (children cannot have honey until after one year)

For the chocolate topping
50ml organic agave nectar
100ml organic cold-pressed coconut oil
50g raw cacao

◆ Rinse your seeds or nuts and put in a food processor with the coconut and dates and make a dough. Press it into a greased 26cm ceramic cake mould. Pop it in the freezer and make the second layer.
◆ Rinse the cashews and put in your food processor with the remaining ingredients. Work well together.
◆ Take your cake out of the freezer and spread over the first layer. Put it in the freezer again.
◆ Melt the coconut oil by putting the jar in warm water. Mix together all the chocolate topping ingredients.
◆ Take the cake out of your freezer, spread this on top and in the freezer again it goes. After a couple of hours you can enjoy it!

• You could also just melt some dark chocolate and spread it on top.

The lovely cake from Nina

A cake from my lovely cousin, this one you can eat guilt-free and bake on a Monday for your whole family to enjoy!

Makes a 26cm cake
2 apples
2–3 organic eggs
*80ml organic unrefined palm or cane sugar, honey, agave nectar or
    maple syrup*
2 tsp cream of tartar
2 tsp ground cinnamon
100g 70 per cent dark chocolate
3 tbsp chopped walnuts
5 tbsp desiccated coconut
4 tbsp organic wholewheat spelt, buckwheat, rice flour or coconut flour

◆ Heat your oven to 180°C/350°F/Gas 4.
◆ Peel, core and grate or finely chop the apples.
◆ Mix the eggs with the sugar until quite fluffy. Add the apples
   very gently with the rest of the ingredients. Pour into a greased
   26cm cake mould (I use coconut oil to grease it) and bake for
   30–35 minutes.

What is tartar baking powder? Tartar baking powder is the white powder made from cream of tartar (potassium hydrogen tartrate) that crystallises out of solution when grapes are fermented during winemaking. Cream of tartar has been around for a long time. For centuries it has been formed from the sediment left over in barrels after the winemaking process. I make sure I buy a gluten- and aluminium-free tartar baking powder. If you want to use a yeast bread recipe but change it into a tartar baking powder one, you use 1 tsp for each 100g of flour. You can also add to that around 2 tsp of lemon juice to make the bread really resemble a yeast bread.

Date and chocolate cake

Makes a 26cm cake
150g dates, stoned
100g chopped or ground almonds or other nuts
100g dark chocolate or dark mint chocolate, which is also lovely!
⅓ cup raw organic palm or cane sugar or organic agave nectar
3 tbsp wholewheat spelt, almond flour or coconut flour
1 tsp vanilla powder
3 tbsp water
2 organic eggs
1 tsp cream of tartar
Whipped cream and fresh berries, to decorate

◆ Heat your oven to 150°C/300°F/Gas 2.
◆ Finely chop everything (you can grind the almonds slowly in your blender or food processor if you like) and mix everything together in a bowl, then let it stand for 15 minutes.
◆ Spoon into a greased 26cm cake mould and bake for 30–40 minutes.
◆ Let it cool and spread whipped cream on top and decorate with fresh berries and/or fruit.

• I have a young niece who cannot have eggs. When she comes over, I skip the eggs, spelt, water and cream of tartar and bake the cake only for about 15 minutes or so. It is quite a different cake but sincerely delicious as well!

You have had enough

This is a good sentence to use with children to give them a sense of what is enough and what isn't. Use it wisely, though, and when it applies, like when they are eating sweets or want more toys. 'It is enough to eat 10 gummy bears. You can have more on Saturday' or 'You have enough toys at home, honey'. Children are also, in my opinion, very smart, so when we really discuss and explain that happiness does not come with a lot of toys, sweets or whatever, they usually get the idea. They might not like it but they understand. I also often have that talk with my children when they happen to see some advertisements on TV. I explain to them how the world works. Those who manufacture all kinds of stuff – food, toys, cosmetic products or whatever – all try to tell us (lie to us, even, if they have to) that we need their products in order to be happy and beautiful so we will buy them and they will get our money! Kids are often more clever than we think.

Sweets

There comes a time in a child's life when everything seems to revolve around getting sweets. You are lucky if your child never reaches that stage. It usually starts at around ages 6 or 7, and it is very normal. But if you feed your child a good diet of fresh organic natural foods and make sure they eat three to five times a day and that there is enough essential fat and good proteins in the diet, your child will crave sweets much less, if at all. Also if a child is not used to sweets at home, this may never become a problem. I think it is always a good idea when buying sweets for children to buy amounts according to their size. A small child should not eat as much as we would buy for ourselves (if we have a sweet tooth).

The first two or three years it is usually easy to keep sweet things away from children. After that it might be more difficult in terms of birthdays, parties, and so on, where they see that everybody is having a cake or something sweet and don't want to be left out! I do advise you not to restrict sugar, as it can make it and its products even more appealing and alluring for children. Everybody can handle eating a little sugar every now and then. You can decide what you buy at your home but there will be parties and there will be holidays and you can't always control it. Trying to be in control all the time will strain you and make you stressed and your whole family as well. Instead, simply embrace it and, more importantly, do not worry. Our body has an amazing ability to handle all kinds of things, including sugar every now and then. If you want to forbid your child ever to have sweets or sugary things, they are likely to resort to going behind your back one day. It is heart-breaking for a small child to lie to mum or dad. Also, if a child is at a party and cannot have what everybody else is having, they may feel left out. So I advise you to be fair, pick your battles and always try to put yourself in your child's shoes.

A little secret; before birthday parties I usually feed my children something healthy because the healthy food, especially protein and healthy fats, keeps our blood sugar from the typical rise and fall rollercoaster and also it makes us want to eat far less sugary food.

About Bread

Bread that can truly give your child healthy nutrition is bread made from organic whole grains and not the white (never mind the bleached) ones. Whole grains taste so much better than the refined ones; they really have much more flavour. Once you try it, you'll know what I mean. And it is so easy to make bread yourself that contains no yeast. The yeast does not do us much good if we eat too much of it. It can make you feel bloated. Yeast can upset our natural internal flora and therefore it is best eaten in moderation. Making bread with tartar baking powder is so much quicker than using yeast. It literally only takes a few minutes.

I sincerely hope you try all or some of these recipes!

You can always substitute some of the spelt wheat in recipes (around 20 per cent) with ground almonds or almond flour as well as coconut flour. I often grind almonds and desiccated coconut slowly into flour in my blender. The protein and good fat in them help stabilise blood sugar levels.

What is spelt?

Spelt is an ancient grain with a deep, nut-like, slightly sweet flavour, that traces its heritage back long before many wheat hybrids. Many of its benefits come from the fact that it offers a broader spectrum of nutrients compared to many of its cousins in the wheat family, and the fact that it is more easily digested than other gluten grains, since it is water soluble.

Spelt was originally grown in Iran around 5000 to 6000 bc. It has been grown in Europe for over 300 years, and in North America for just over 100 years. Throughout early European history, as populations migrated throughout the continent, they brought this nutritious grain with them to their new lands. Spelt became a popular grain, especially in Switzerland, Germany and Austria. During the Middle Ages, spelt earned another level of recognition with the famous healer Hildegard von Bingen, who used spelt as a panacea for many illnesses.

Spelt was introduced to the United States in the 1890s. But in the 20th century, spelt was replaced by wheat in almost all areas where it was still grown. One of the reasons for this agricultural shift is that spelt's nutrient-rich tough husk makes it harder to process than wheat. This tough husk may help protect the nutrients in spelt and make it easier to grow without the use of pesticides.

Recently this ancient grain has regained popularity with organic farmers as a dietary grain, because spelt requires fewer fertilisers and has maintained its purity since it was forgotten when they started genetically modifying wheat in the beginning of the 20th century.

Spelt contains more protein (17%) than wheat and the protein is far easier to digest. This means that some people who are sensitive to wheat and wheat products tolerate spelt well. Spelt is used in the same way as wheat for example in breads, cookies and pasta.

Store spelt grains in an airtight container in a cool, dry and dark place. Spelt flour should be kept in the refrigerator to best preserve its nutritional value.

You can always substitute the spelt flour with organic kamut or durum wheat, for example. Also keep in mind that wholegrain flour absorbs more liquid than the finely milled flour. You can always add a little warm water if your dough is too dry and more flour if it is too wet!

Spelt pan bread

Quick and easy to make and utterly delicious, this is a recipe from Raw Solla. I have used this one for so many years with my soups and stews.

Makes about 10 pieces
150g organic whole spelt flour or organic wholewheat flour
1 tsp sea salt
2 tbsp cold-pressed coconut or olive oil
100ml hot water

◆ Blend the spelt and the sea salt in a bowl. Add the oil and the water and make a dough with your hands. Roll the dough and cut it into 10 pieces. Put a little spelt on your table and flatten each piece quite thinly using the inside of your palms or a rolling pin.
◆ Then you simply cook them dry (no oil or water) on a pan for about 1 minute each side. Watch the heat, I keep it low!

• You can also bake them in the oven at around 180°C/350°F/Gas 4 on a lined baking sheet.
• When ready to serve, I love olive oil or garlic olive oil on my bread and just a little Himalayan salt.
• You can easily also put around 2 tbsp ground seeds into this recipe. I grind mine using low speed in my blender.
• You can also substitute up to 40 per cent of the spelt flour with buckwheat flour.

Spelt scones

This takes you 10 minutes to prepare and then the scones are off to the oven!

Makes 12–15
350g wholewheat spelt flour (or whole and fine fifty/fifty)
1 tsp sea salt
2 tsp ground cardamom
4 tsp cream of tartar
200ml warm organic rice milk or other milk you like
5 tbsp organic soft cold-pressed coconut oil, olive oil or melted butter

◆ Heat your oven to 180°C/350°F/Gas 4.
◆ Mix the dry ingredients together. Warm the organic rice milk. Add the rest of the ingredients and make dough with your hands. Using your hands, make around 15 scones.
◆ Put them on a baking tray lined with greaseproof paper and bake them for around 15–17 minutes, depending on their size, until they are light golden brown.

• I love mine with blueberry jam and cucumber.
• You may like to add some raisins or other dried fruit to the dough.
• Be careful not to knead spelt dough too much; it can become chewy and difficult to handle if you do.

Naan bread

Makes 4

*250g organic pure yoghurt or Greek yoghurt (You can also use coconut
milk and 2 tbsp of lemon juice)*
2 tbsp organic honey
330g organic spelt flour (I use whole and fine fifty/fifty)
2 tsp cream of tartar

♦ Heat your oven to 180°C/350°F/Gas 6.
♦ Mix the yoghurt and honey. Then add the other ingredients and
  make a dough (I use a spoon and then my hands). Add hot
  water if needed.
♦ Make around 5mm thick cakes with your hands, using a little
  fine spelt to prevent sticking (shape and size does not matter).
  You can also put a little fine spelt on your table and flatten each
  piece quite thinly using the inside of your palms or a rolling pin.
♦ Bake them on a lined baking sheet for around 10 minutes.

My Grandma's bread

It takes you 5 minutes to prepare this bread and then it is off to the oven. You can use whole spelt and fine spelt fifty/fifty, you can also substitute 50g spelt with desiccated coconut.

Makes a medium loaf
3 cups wholewheat spelt flour
4 tsp cream of tartar
1 tsp sea salt
2 tbsp organic raw honey
250ml warm water
120ml organic pure yoghurt, organic milk, rice milk or almond milk

◆ Heat your oven to 180°C/350°F/Gas 4.
◆ Mix the dry ingredients together and then add the honey and the warm water. Next, add the yoghurt or milk. Mix together gently but be careful not to stir too much. The dough should resemble a very thick porridge.
◆ Bake in a greased or lined 900g bread tin (I put coconut oil inside the mould to prevent sticking or baking paper) for about 30–35 minutes.
◆ Take the bread out of the tin and bake it 'naked' for further 5–10 minutes or so.

• When you have made the dough, you could also add olives, sundried tomatoes or any spices you like to the dough.
• You can also put this bread (as any other) into muffin moulds and bake it for a shorter period of time then, around 15 minutes.
• You can put 2–3 ripe mashed bananas into the bread instead of the honey and make a banana bread!
• You can add seeds and nuts you like into your bread.

> If the coconut oil is solid, you simply put the amount you need for the recipe in a glass jar and the jat in hot water (no warmer than 40°C/100°F) and then it soon becomes runny enough for you to use in your recipe. You can also melt it in a pan using a low heat like you would with butter.

Yeast-free cheese bread
Bake this wonderful bread in muffin cases.

Makes 12–15
350g wholewheat spelt flour
3 tsp cream of tartar
1 tsp sea salt
100–200ml warm water (start with 100ml and add as needed)
100g full-fat organic cheese you love, grated
1 organic egg (optional)
3 tbsp organic cold-pressed olive oil
200ml coconut milk (I get it in cartons with no preservatives,
  thickeners, etc.) or other milk you like
1–2 garlic cloves

◆ Heat your oven to 180°C/350°F/Gas 4.
◆ Mix the spelt, cream of tartar and sea salt and then pour over it
  the warm water. Add the cheese and blend a little.
◆ In another bowl, blend together the egg, olive oil, coconut milk
  and pressed garlic clove. Now blend everything together and
  add hot water if you need it. The dough should resemble a
  sticky, thick porridge. Pour into lined muffin tins and bake for
  around 15 minutes.

• We love dipping those warm into cold-pressed olive oil and
  himalaya- or sea salt.
• What is also lovely is to mix together one part organic ketchup,
  one part organic tomato paste and one part organic red pesto
  along with a splash of olive oil and serve with those to dip in.

What can you put on your bread?

Just use your imagination! But here are some ideas to get you started.

- Organic butter.
- Organic olive oil and Himalaya/sea salt.
- Organic raw coconut oil.
- Hummus.
- Pesto.
- Cucumber.
- Apple.
- Banana.
- Jam (I often buy ones that are sweetened with fruit juices).
- Almond spread or other nut/seed butter (tahini) and jam or a banana.
- Tomatoes (after your baby is one year).
- Hard-boiled eggs.
- Organic honey (after your baby is one year).

In short, endless possibilities.

Other Important Ingredients

Here is a little more information on some of the nutritious and delicious ingredients I use in my cooking.

Seeds

Hemp seeds, sunflower seeds, sesame seeds, chia seeds, pumpkin seeds and flax seeds are all examples of edible seeds. Seeds are filled with vitamins, proteins and healthy fats. Seeds can, for example, be ground with a grinder and put into the porridge for babies from 8 months. Fat makes up around 50 per cent of all seeds and therefore they must be ground shortly before they are consumed; they become rancid quite quickly after being ground. All fat-rich food – such as seeds, almonds, nuts and oils – are subject to rancidity over time. The best thing to do is to store those in closed containers away from heat or light at all times to increase their life and avoid loss of nutrients.

For easier digestion, it is recommended that you soak your seeds overnight. The next morning you can easily put them in your smoothie, baby purée or on your porridge but always remember to rinse the seeds after soaking and discard the water they were soaked in.

Babies can have ground seeds from 8 months, ground almonds from 9 months and ground nuts from one year old, although I do not recommend peanuts for children in general. Please keep in mind that nuts should be treated more carefully if there is a history of nut allergy in the family.

Babies should not be allowed to consume whole nuts until they are chewing properly. The age varies, of course, between children but for many it is not until they are 4 years old.

Nuts

Like seeds, nuts are a great source of nutrients, proteins and healthy fats. Nut proteins are known for being more digestible than animal proteins. Nut allergy is quite common and therefore it is recommended that babies should not have nuts until they are at least 12 months old. However, babies can have almonds from the age of 9 months but they must be puréed and consumed as smoothies, sieved 'milk' or shakes. Without a doubt, almonds (and later nuts) with all its nutrients and good fats are an important source of energy not only for small babies but also for older children who are more active.

Nuts can easily be used for smoothies and shakes but one can also buy various purées made from nuts. My personal favourites are the hazelnut purée, macadamia purée and almond purée which I love to have with, for example, apples and many love it on bread or crackers with jam.

> Baking paper is wonderful to use between your sandwiches in the lunch box. It does not give back any unhealthy stuff into your food like some plastic does.

Yoghurt

I recommend organic non-flavoured yoghurt or Greek yoghurt for those who choose to give their children dairy products. It can be given to them when they have reached 12 months, about one portion a day (one meal, yoghurt meal). Yoghurt contains the good bacteria for the intestine flora and you can mix many different flavours with pure yoghurt that are not overly sweetened with white sugar. If the label states that the dairy product has no added sugar, check if any sweetener (nutrasweet or aspartam) is added. I, myself, do not like sweeteners. I never buy anything with them in it.

Suggestions for ingredients to add to pure organic yoghurt:
- Nothing! It s very sensible to regularly give babies pure yoghurt so they get used to it.
- Organic sugar-free jam (with no sweeteners).
- Fruit purée, puréed fruits that you prepare yourself or buy.
- Puréed dried fruits (cooked or soaked and then puréed).
- Sugar beet syrup (just use very little).

- Vanilla powder.
- Almond purée.
- Organic white tahini.
- Linseed or hemp oil (for the omega-3).
- Soaked chia seeds (for the omega-3).

When you are tired, tense, lonely or unhappy, it can change everything if you just put on some music and dance like a maniac. It relaxes you and makes you happy! And your kids will also love it!

Dried fruits

As you can see in many of the recipes in this book, there are many sweet things that you can use for your kids, big and small, instead of sugar. I like dried fruits and they are very nutritious, just like fresh fruits. (Make sure they have not been handled with sulphur dioxide.) Some vitamins, however, like vitamin C, are destroyed during the drying process. Vitamin C is a very delicate vitamin. It is quickly destroyed when it comes in touch with light, oxygen, heat or water.

There are many options when it comes to dried fruits. You can get raisins (I recommend organic sultanas or raisins), dried mango, apricots, pineapple, banana, prunes, apple, dates, figs, goji berries and so on. It is a good idea to bring with you a small box of dried fruits when you are going somewhere special because kids usually like munching on them and are in no need of sweets if they have dried fruits. It is good, however, to bear in mind that you should give dried fruits in moderation like anything else that is sweet.

I love the South African super fruit Baobab, which you can buy in powder form. It has double the antioxidants of cranberries and pomegranates, more than three times more than blueberries and ten times more than oranges. It is also a significant source of iron, potassium and magnesium and has a higher level of calcium than milk but is far easier to absorb and digest. I use it a lot in my shakes for my family.

Breakfast cereal

There is a great selection in health food stores of organic breakfast cereals that are without additives, only processed from whole grains (I personally love the gluten-free ones like buckwheat and amaranth) and sweetened with honey or raw cane sugar. You can also buy them unsweetened. I truly recommend this kind of breakfast cereal rather than the regular ones. If kids get used to it from the start, they like it. It is harder to go from overly sweetened breakfast cereal to a healthier one, which is not as sweet and made from what they might perceive as an 'exotic' grain type.

Older children, salad and vegetables

As your child starts chewing properly, I recommend offering lots and lots of salad and raw vegetables and fruits. I am positive that children whose parents wash, peel and cut fruits and vegetables for them, eat more than those whose parents don't. Cutting vegetables into strips is also a nice way for children to munch on them. Children cannot grow accustomed to things they never see or experience, so having a new small person at the dinner table is a golden opportunity to start offering salad and raw vegetables as often as possible, since it sometimes becomes harder with age to get children to taste new foods.

You could sometimes throw the vegetables into boiling water for 5 seconds, which makes it warm and clean but keeps all its nutrients. Bear in mind that parents are their children's role models and children are far more likely to taste and eat what they see their parents eating. And believe you me, very green broccoli, red tomatoes and peppers and orange carrots, for instance, look oh so pretty on the dinner table. All these beautiful colours indicate nutrients. But don't get me wrong, you don't have to offer everything at each meal, broccoli today and tomatoes tomorrow is just fine and very doable!

A Healthy Lifestyle

Food is just one element of a healthy lifestyle but an essential one. In this chapter we will look at just some of the aspects of a healthy lifestyle, and some of the health issues you may experience.

Eating regularly

I think it is almost as important to teach children to eat regularly as to eat healthily. Children need a breakfast, lunch, mid-day snack, dinner and also maybe a healthy light evening snack, like fruits that are very easily digested and do not prevent us from sleeping well. It is better for our body not to sleep on a full stomach because while we sleep our body is trying to rest and restore itself, and it cannot do that if it is digesting too much food.

When children do not want to eat

I remember when my daughter was around 2½ years old, she thought it was very exciting if I told her that her tongue would become green if she ate green vegetables. She then ate her greens and immediately showed me her tongue and I, of course, became so surprised how green it was! When my kids were babies, I sometimes allowed them to draw a picture or look through a book during meals when they did not want to eat anything (and I knew they had to be hungry). Sometimes when I knew they didn't fancy what was for dinner, I gave them as a side dish a few cut dates, apple bits, whole spelt pasta or other things I knew they liked but which weren't unhealthy – something to bring them to the table (something to bribe them with). They would then eat one mouthful of what was for dinner and one of the food they really like, and thus I got them to eat their meal.

It can also help at a certain age to talk about how big and strong they will become if they eat this or that, or how fast they will run, how high they will be able to jump or other ideas you know will raise their interest. You can also ask them to eat for someone, like

Grandma, the moon, the birds, the dog next door (if they like it), Santa Claus. Furthermore you can call the food names and pick names of favourite persons, idols, cartoon characters or whatever you can think of, to try to tempt them. When my son was around 2 years old and didn't want to eat, I sometimes managed to give him a few bites by clapping a lot and saying real loudly 'Yay!' when he opened his mouth. Sometimes it can work to compete with them, but just give them very little on the plate if you know they do not like the food. A huge portion can make a child give up before they even start eating, so keep portions small. It is better to give them the opportunity to ask for seconds.

It is very positive to have family meals, where everybody sits down and dines together at the same time. Try to do this at least once a day. Then your kids will have role models (you) eating healthy food, everybody together, discussing their day. It is a very enjoyable family tradition, something to look forward to every day, and it also relaxes you. Parents should also try to eat slowly and enjoy their dinner for their children to see. This is not a time to discuss fad diets, for example. Actually I don't think it is a good idea that parents talk about fat/thin issues in front of their children. If you eat healthy food you feel good and you pretty much keep your ideal weight.

I would like to stress that positive encouragement works so much better than shouting and yelling. If your child simply does not want to eat anything maybe there is a reason for it. I know kids. for example, who have never wanted to eat meat. Maybe they are just not meant to eat meat. We are not all the same. Think before you shout. It is said that children need to be offered food they do not like eight or ten times before they want to eat it. Being a parent really shows you what you are made of in terms of patience and tolerance! (And just for the record I have shouted at meal time, although I am not proud of it.) Also bear in mind that it is not realistic that a child eats a full plate of something it just started eating or just agreed to trying; so again, small portions.

Allowing your kids to help you in the kitchen also might result in less fussy eaters. Also remember to praise when they eat or taste new foods without complaints (positive reinforcement).

Last but not least, when children are small and do not want to eat their dinner, it may be that the dinner is simply being served too late for them. Sometimes it is better to have dinner earlier, between five and six. in other words, at a time when they are not too tired to eat. It also matters that the child is hungry. If a child has been given a glass of milk or juice just before dinner, not to mention biscuits or sweets, it is very understandable that they won't want to eat dinner. They aren't hungry.

However, if your child is never hungry and never wants to eat, you should consult a doctor. Iron deficiency can result in lack of appetite, restlessness and tiredness. Reflux can also result in a child not wanting to eat since most of the food comes back up again with acid (which means the child probably also has trouble sleeping). Lack of zinc is also said to reduce appetite and disturb both sense of smell and taste. Bear in mind as well that children are often more clever and sensible than we give them credit for. You can often discuss with older children in all serenity about healthy food and why you want them to eat as much as they can of it, why some foods are Saturday or weekend/holiday foods and others are day-to-day foods.

It is very normal for children to eat a lot today and less tomorrow and so on and so forth. Their calorie intake often varies from day to day. It will all balance out in the end.

Going out with a small child

I always take some snacks with me when I go out with my children. Often there are not any healthy options available when you are away from home. Furthermore, small children don't easily tolerate being hungry and become frustrated and can even start to cry. It is very easy to take some snacks and water with you when going out for the day.

When you have small babies, I recommend purées in a cool bag and some water to drink. Water is always the most important thing. As they get older you can grab some cut fruits, vegetables, almonds, dried fruits, even wholewheat bread or cooked pasta. You can also take with you a shake that you've made. Anything is possible and this saves money, time and gives you healthy energy wherever you or your children need it. A cool bag is therefore a must-have, especially where the climate can be very hot.

Instead of using the store-bought wet tissues on your baby's bottoms you can easily make your own which are then free of any unwanted substances. You simply wet a few gauzes with water, cold-pressed oil (jojoba, olive or chamomile oil, for example) and lavender essential oil. Keep this in an airtight container and take it with you when travelling. It is good also to clean dirty hands as well as bottoms!

When travelling

It is very sensible to take healthy food with you when going on a fun journey. Children are often very conventional and don't like to experience new things like new food. Also, when travelling to new places we often have no clue where this and that can be bought so this can possibly save us a lot of trouble. I remember taking organic baby food (homemade or jars) with me that would last the first days at least while I was trying to find out where to buy things at a new place. But I do not recommend liquids among your clothes when going on an aeroplane. That could end badly unless you pack it really well. I also recommend taking cold-pressed oil with you to put into baby food (I kept it in a Ziploc bag). My kids have always loved carrot juice so I very often took that with me as well. Even some good-quality spelt bread or gluten-free bread can be very convenient to take with to have for the first two days, and maybe rice crackers. All this has always come in handy.

I also usually take with me my glass measuring jug and hand-held blender along with some extra zipper bags and some BPA-free plastic containers, my high-quality, food-grade, stainless steel water bottle and my cool bag.

I use a lot of lavender essential oil so therefore that goes with me everywhere. It is great to disinfect wounds (or dirty hands) and it calms the skin when burned or if rashes occur. It is also great on mosquito bites and is also an excellent fly and bug repellent, although eucalyptus and lemongrass also do the job there. I also take them with me everywhere!

For older children I also recommend taking wholewheat spelt pasta to boil for them and some nice organic tomato sauce. Also, sometimes I bring brown rice, oats or quinoa because all these are easy to boil (or soak) to make a quick and healthy breakfast, lunch or dinner.

My experience is that eating nutritious, whole food helps you eat less because your body becomes full sooner when eating nutritious calories as opposed to empty calories, meaning calories without any nutritional value. This also means that even though healthy food sometimes costs more than unhealthy options, you need less of the healthy food. I also have found out that I really make sure that nothing is wasted when I buy good quality food. Not wasting food is very positive for everybody because it is a huge problem, especially in the Western world, how much food is thrown away. We would not have to grow so much and put so much strain on our eco-system if we only bought what we needed.

Supplements for babies

When babies and children are eating a varied diet of fresh fruits and vegetables, whole grains and good essential fats, seeds and nuts, lentils, beans or meat, organic milk products (in moderation), they probably do not have any need for supplements. However, I do believe that green superfood supplements do us all good and can be taken every now and then. You can buy organic pure wheat grass, spirulina, chlorella or blue green algae in powder form, for instance. This can be mixed in very small quantities (½ tsp) into shakes or juices for your baby. You can also buy great-tasting green superfood supplements specially formulated for kids. Green superfood has a very concentrated quantity of nutrients per amount. And since this is something that our nature gives us the body knows exactly how to utilise it, which is not always the case with synthetic multi vitamins.

Did you know that lemons are actually alkalizing for your body? They contain a lot of vitamin C and act as a natural preservative. They also bring out the flavour in food and have disinfecting properties. When your child is one year old, you can sometimes squeeze a little lemon into his or her food. Vitamin C also helps the body utilise iron and it helps your body fight infections.

When your kids are sick

When your children are sick, it is normal if they do not have much of an appetite. You should not worry about that. The most important thing is to give them plenty of water and/or organic coconut water. You could also give them well-diluted pure fruit juices (1 part juice and 4 parts water) and maybe healthy shakes you prepare yourself. You can also freeze shakes and diluted juice in lollipop moulds. Our body always tries to heal itself and uses up a lot of energy when doing so and, since digestion takes up a lot of energy too, it is very good to eat easily digested foods when sick. That means, for example, fruits and vegetables and, of course, lots of water.

> I myself used homeopathic remedies successfully for my children when they were little. It is worth the shot if a child is not dangerously ill. It could prevent the use of antibiotics for example which is good since they should best be used in emergencies.

Antibiotics

When my children have had to use antibiotics, I have always given them acidophilus supplements. You can buy acidophilus in most health stores. When buying acidophilus for your small baby you should buy the one specially formulated for small babies (infant acidophilus!) and it is best in powder form that mixes well in all beverages. This is important because a baby's intestinal flora is different from that of an adult.

Acidophilus can help to protect the body against harmful bacteria, parasites and other organisms. The term acidophilus is used to describe a number of friendly bacteria that help in human digestion and are found naturally throughout the human body. These bacteria include *Lactobacilus acidophilus, L. casei, L. bulgaricus,* among others. *L. acidophilus* is one of the strains of bacteria found in these mixtures, but the term acidophilus usually refers to a combination of *L. acidophilus* with other beneficial bacteria.

Antibiotics kill the harmful bacteria that are making us ill. The bad news is that they also kill our very essential good bacteria, the so-called probiotics. Therefore, ingesting supplements of acidophilus when using antibiotics is a great idea to prevent yeast infections. But you should not take acidophilus until at least an hour before or after you take antibiotics for the acidophilus to work properly. Furthermore I would give it long after you or your baby finish the antibiotics. Many researches indicate that a healthy intestinal flora is a solid foundation for good health and some even go further and say that all illnesses begin in our digestive track. Acidophilus is therefore used to help bolster the immune system as a whole.

Fungal infection of *Candida albicans*, often referred to as a yeast infection, can be treated with ingesting acidophilus 2–3 times a day for a few months. But if one is suffering from a bad yeast infection it is wise to cut out sugar, wheat and yeast as this is 'food' that feeds the fungus. I would also limit milk products and gluten for a while. Diarrhoea and rash on your baby's bottom for instance can be an indicator of a mild yeast infection.

Diarrhoea

If your child has diarrhoea it is very important to give them water to counteract the loss of fluid from the body. Coconut water would also be great. And you can also dilute fruit juices with water or coconut water. A homemade healthy shake is something that your child might also enjoy when sick and you can also freeze them in lollipop moulds and serve them as an ice-cream. Brown rice, organic rice milk, carrots and blueberries are all anti-diarrhoeal. I would also suggest feeding your child acidophilus to help build up and maintain healthy intestinal flora. Diarrhoea can also be a symptom of food intolerance.

Always remember to take a break from each superfood every 4 weeks or so for a about a week or so.

Constipation

If your child is suffering from constipation it is very important to make sure he or she drinks a lot of water. You can also dilute fruit juice with water every now and then to have your baby drink more. I would also try to put hemp seed oil into the diluted fruit juice and preferably try to feed your child 1 tsp hemp oil, linseed oil, coconut oil or olive oil three or four times a day before or with meals. Cold-pressed oils really help soften stools, as does an avocado and chia seeds! You can put some chia seeds into water for your baby to drink. Prunes are also a great natural laxative. They can be puréed with some fruits, for instance, or simply eaten directly by older children. Just make sure they are stoned.

Try to limit all milk products, since they tend to be encourage constipation, and also white processed goods like white wheat and white sugar (which should, of course, be limited always since they do not offer any nutritional value). Offer your child plenty of fibre-rich natural foods like vegetables, fruits and whole grains, especially quinoa and oats. Chia seeds and avocado are especially good since they contain so much of the good fat, which softens stools. You can easily make healthy shakes for your baby to enjoy and use Chia seeds and/or avocados in them as well as hempseed oil, coconut oil, almonds, seeds etc. Almonds, nuts and seeds are rich in fibre, full of good fats, nutrients and still quite a light energy since they are very easily digested. Shakes are furthermore easier on the stomach since they have already been puréed, which helps the digestion. Also, in my experience, oat milk can help children who are constipated. I would also suggest ½–1tsp infant/children's acidophilus, two or three times a day.

A child who cannot pass stools very often does not want to eat, so it is important to really try to sort out the problem. Try to avoid using laxatives if possible. There is always some underlying cause that should be addressed. Magnesium is a natural laxative. You can buy that in powder form to mix with a little hot water. You can then mix the hot water with a little fruit juice and give to your child. Just remember always to follow the instructions very carefully.

You can use stories to make your children do things like go to the toilet. I used to tell mine that the poo needed to go home to the sea. My children always asked, very intrigued, 'to see his mum and dad?' and I, of course, just said, 'yes indeed'.

> If your child is unwell, you should always seek appropriate medical advice.

Iron deficiency

Having enough iron can help us fight infections and thus helps us maintain a healthy immune system.

Iron is a mineral that is found in every cell in the body. We need the correct amount of iron in our body because iron is used by blood cells to carry oxygen to all other cells in the body. Enough iron can thus help us fight infections because it keeps the immune system healthy and it also helps brain cells function normally.

In short, iron assists the transport of oxygen around the body, helps fight infection and is used in energy production.

Iron deficiency is one of the most common nutritional deficiencies in the world. Iron deficiency can be caused by several factors including not getting enough iron in one's diet, not absorbing iron properly and losing blood from injury or illness. You can also gradually lose blood over time through menstruation. Without adequate iron, red blood cells cannot carry enough oxygen to other cells in the body.

Processed food like white wheat, sweets, fizzy drinks and commercially made ice-cream, for instance, which all contain a lot of preservatives and all kinds of unnatural additives, can limit iron absorption, as does calcium. It is best to not eat or drink calcium-rich foods, like dairy products, with iron-rich foods. Vitamin C, on the other hand, enhances iron absorption.

You will find iron in all very dark green salad/leaves, broccoli, bok choy, red beets, whole grains, dried apricots, prunes, raisins, flax seeds, sesame seeds, pumpkin seeds, lentils, beans, almonds, berries, yolk and red meat. And vitamin C is found in dark leafy greens, broccoli, cauliflower, brussels sprouts, peppers, lemons and limes, kiwi fruits, guavas, fresh parsley, papaya, oranges and strawberries to name a few.

Symptoms of iron deficiency are tiredness, depression, limited attention span, difficulty focusing, hyperactivity, poor mental ability, lack of appetite and just in short you always feel under the weather. It is not nice, I speak from experience.

Beware of iron supplements. A child only needs to swallow a few of them for it to be life threatening. Keep them safe away from children's reach. After a child is 12 months old, you can buy iron-rich fluids in health stores that are made using only natural ingredients. These could be considered if you or your child are lacking in iron.

Natural Fibres for Babies

For those of you who are unaware, I wanted to tell you why silk and wool are wonderful materials! Since my children were born, I have dressed them in silk and woollen underwear and hats, and I still do to this day (they are now 7 and 10 years old). My son gets warm very easily, but regardless he is always quick to reach for his mixed wool and silk undergarments.

About silk hats for babies

A silk hat protects the baby's scalp, as well as its sensitive hearing from constant noises in the environment. The soft texture of a silk hat feels good against the baby s head, and can give them a sense of calm and security. The size of a baby s head is relatively large in comparison to the rest of the body, so a drop in temperature in the head can be serious, but the protection of the silk hat helps the baby maintain a constant temperature. Babies can wear the hat day or night since, due to the unique properties of silk, it holds in warmth when it is cold, and at the same time it can have a cooling effect when it is warm.

Silk contains the nourishing protein sericin, which can reduce skin irritation. The properties of silk are actually quite similar to that of human skin, which explains why it is often referred to as a 'second skin'. Silk is a very warm material, almost comparable to wool, and it is five times warmer than cotton. Silk threads withhold enough air to function as thermal insulation, but thanks to the fine and light strand of silk it is not only colder than wool but also great in hot weather (has a cooling effect!).

Wool

During wintertime and in colder regions of the world (such as Iceland), temperatures can drop drastically. In such weather, we tend to layer up in sweaters and other clothing that protects us from the cold. When we sweat from being active, cotton underwear is an unfortunate and inconvenient choice of undergarment, since the cotton absorbs sweat and moisture from the body, and underwear can become soggy, and even wet. The moisture in the underwear then guides heat away from the body, and attracts coldness towards the body, which can result in hypothermia (shivering and feeling very cold). The more a child is layered up in clothing, the more moisture there will be in cotton underwear. Moisture in cotton underwear furthermore enhances the formation of fungi and bacteria on the skin. Moisture against the skin can also reduce the oxygen flow. The consequences of this lack of oxygen can, for example, result in redness or scabs caused by fungi and bacteria. These symptoms are rapidly diminished with the use of woollen undergarments.

It is also believed that the bacteria that cause ear diseases are more likely to harm the child if cotton hats are worn. Silk or woollen

hats that are in close contact with the scalp are a better choice. Woollen underwear has the opposite effect, because moisture from the body will not be absorbed into the wool thread as it does with the cotton thread, but rather it evaporates out of the garment with the help of heat emission from the body. When selecting woollen underwear, it is important to consider the type of wool, because this can vary depending on the sheep. In general, the smaller it is, the softer the wool will be. Merino wool (from Merino sheep) is one of the best wools available, and it is important that it has received organic treatment from start to finish. It should also always be washed with organic soap only. Merino wool is soft and actually becomes warmer when it is moist, which makes it a great under garment when staying out for a long period of time and/or on long travels. Merino wool does not retain bad body odour, since the skin is given enough oxygen so it can better defend itself against fungi and bacteria.

Some people are allergic to wool, but in these cases 100 per cent silk underwear does the trick. Silk is even more bacteria- and fungi-repellant than wool.

> Stress is poison. It is very important for all of us, both adults and children, to get adequate rest along with peace and quiet regularly to unwind and relax. A heavy programme and too much work threatens our immune system. And what helps keep our immune system healthy are happy thoughts, forgiveness, gratefulness, optimism, laughter and love. And it is actually easy to teach children these things. When they start going off about how unlucky they are not to have this or that or that they cannot do this or that, we can step in and tell them about all the things they are so lucky to have in their life and how grateful they should be. It is life-threatening to be consumed with self-pity and negative thoughts. So this actually gives them tools they can use themselves later on, to be happy and grateful.

Indexes